Reyner Banham
A Set of Actual Tracks

AA Publications   **Edited by Ludovico Centis**

p 4–9
Ludovico Centis
Introduction

p 10–20
Barbara Penner
Mies in the Lavatory
Reyner Banham: *The Last Professional*
in *New Society*

p 21–46
Penny Sparke
The Dream of Technology
Reyner Banham: *The Great Gizmo*
in *Industrial Design*

p 47–64
Mario Carpo
From Softer Hardware to Software
Reyner Banham: *Softer Hardware*
in *ARK – Journal of the Royal College of Art*

p 73–91
Mimi Zeiger
Cheeseburger in Paradise
Reyner Banham: *Architecture II: Fantastic*
in *Los Angeles: The Architecture of Four Ecologies*

p 92–105
Richard J Williams
The 'Spectacular Paradox' of Autopia
Reyner Banham: *Ecology IV: Autopia*
in *Los Angeles: The Architecture of Four Ecologies*

p 106–23
Paola Viganò
The Historian of the Total Artefact
Reyner Banham: *Ecology II: Foothills*
in *Los Angeles: The Architecture of Four Ecologies*

p 124–52
Curt Gambetta
I Was There
Reyner Banham: *Introduction*
in *A Concrete Atlantis: U.S. Industrial Building and European Modern Architecture*

p 153–62
Alice Twemlow
Banham's Pedagogy on the Page
Reyner Banham: *O, Bright Star...*
in *New Society*

p 163–6
Kersten Geers
Giving and Taking
Reyner Banham: *Revelation*
in *Scenes in America Deserta*

p 167–80
Albert Narath
Solar Futures Past: Banham on Baer
Reyner Banham: *The Sage of Corrales*
in *New Society*

p 181–95
Tim Street-Porter
Travels with Banham
Reyner Banham: *The Architecture of Silicon Valley*
in *New West*

p 196–206
Adrian Forty
Wordless in Zzyzx
Reyner Banham: The last pages of *Scenes in America Deserta*

p 207–11
Ludovico Centis
A Farewell to Words
Reyner Banham: *The Wall* in *SAH Newsletter*

p 212–5
Oliver Arditi
The Elision of Geography

p 216–9
Maristella Casciato
Afterword: Reyner Banham Then and Now

p 220–3
Biographies

p 224–7
Acknowledgements

Ludovico Centis
Introduction

Peter Reyner Banham produced memorable openings. One of them, introducing the essay 'The Wilderness Years of Frank Lloyd Wright', resonates with this anthology and research at large:

'"Let us now praise famous men in chronological order". Really, the keeping of centenaries is among the dottier rituals of Western culture. The purely numerical magic of 10×10 drives us to comb the works of famous artists, politicians, architects, plaintively inquiring: "What survives of his achievement 100 years later?" Since this is a purely rhetorical question, deserving the answer "Who cares?", the centenary orator hurries to ward off this vulgar riposte by inventing achievements that had not been noticed before. [...] So, why am I bothering to play the centenary game? Because I think there are some things that did, factually, happen in Wright's career but which have eluded historical understanding and critical attention.'[1]

Indeed, these lines frame very well Banham's wit and way of operating, which brought attention back to topics and issues, as well as objects, buildings, cities and landscapes, that he felt had been largely forgotten, overlooked or even despised. The vastness and relevance of his intellectual legacy – from hundreds of articles and essays to milestone books and innovative pedagogical experiences such as 'The Time and Place of Your Life', which he taught at The Bartlett School of Architecture with Adrian Forty, and the 'Building Life Cycles' programme he ran at the State University of New York at Buffalo with Beverly Foit-Albert – already provides a convincing answer about why we should care about his work.

This self-initiated six-year-long project, titled *Reyner Banham: A Set of Actual Tracks*, also afforded the opportunity to play the centenary game – in Banham's words – through a symposium held at the Architectural Association in London on 4 March 2022 titled *What Happens on your 100th Birthday? A Set of Confabulations in Memory of Peter Reyner Banham*, from which this book emerges. The unfolding of both the symposium and the broader project has given me and a wider group of scholars and practitioners the chance to investigate and question Banham's attitude and work methods through a fresh critical lens. This research effort is not simply an exercise in revealing lesser-known texts and episodes of Banham's life, but in engaging with his work, testing its validity and points of weakness, and producing new texts that establish a dialogue with Reyner Banham's brilliant, multifaceted and occasionally elusive legacy.

Some key suggestions for how to relate to his work derive from what we might consider Banham's unintended final testament, 'Actual Monuments'.[2] This poignant text was conceived as a never-delivered inaugural lecture as the Sheldon H Solow Chair of the History of Architecture at the Institute of Fine Arts, New York University, in 1988. Here, Banham analysed the legacy of his predecessor at New York University, architectural historian Henry-Russell Hitchcock, as well as Hitchcock's role in introducing modernism to the United States in the first half of the 20th century. We learn some fundamental things about Banham in this text: he considered himself to belong to a group of 'observational historians' – as Nikolaus Pevsner and Henry-Russell Hitchcock did before him – who related to what Robert Maxwell referred to as the 'rhetoric of presence': the idea that the license, the authority to speak about something, comes first from experiencing it, from having seen it with your own eyes.[3] Banham's extensive ground exploration is closely related to this rhetoric of presence. In his practice, fieldwork on site acted as a validation – or sometimes as a contradiction – of archival research or information contained in secondary sources. The ground exploration sometimes evolved into something deeper, a sort of 'architectural archaeology',[4] as in the case of the research run by Banham and some of his UC Santa Cruz students at Ocatillo Camp, Arizona, in the 1980s.[5]

Banham took the occasion to recall the notion of 'actual monuments', which stood at the core of Hitchcock's milestone book *The International Style*[6], to define a fundamental triad when dealing with the history and theory of architecture:

'For not only does architecture consist of a set of actual monuments, its history also consists of a set of actual books; and of course a set of actual historians'.[7]

Banham has left us a tremendously rich set not only of books that we can consider as monuments in the evolution of the history of architecture, but also of tracks. These tracks are both intellectual and spatialised. His intellectual tracks have been disseminated in a constellation of essays and articles published in magazines and books throughout several decades, as well as recordings and transcripts from events such as the Aspen Design Conference that Banham eagerly attended for many years or his participation in innovative educational experiences such as the Open University. Banham's spatialised tracks derive from ground explorations that are part of a well-established tradition of road trips and fieldwork in North America, famously upheld by writers and artists such as Jack Kerouac, William Least Heat-Moon, Ed Ruscha and Lee Friedlander. This kind of ritual has also been taken up by Europeans, including artists, scholars and thinkers who produced seminal works and texts after their trips, including Robert Frank, Simone de Beauvoir and Jean Baudrillard.

    The fertile and tangled relationship between Europe and North America, the United States in particular, is obviously part of Banham's biography, given that he visited the US multiple times for conferences and fieldwork before settling first in 1976 in Buffalo, New York, and then later in 1980 in Santa Cruz, California. This relationship stood also at the core of his research – the book *A Concrete Atlantis: U.S. Industrial Building and European Modern Architecture 1900-1925* is a clear example in this sense – and sometimes resulted in problematic and often unsolved tensions, as Banham's grandson Oliver Arditi's contribution, 'The Elision of Geography', testifies.

    I took this same relationship between Europe and North America into account to draft the list of speakers who took part in the symposium of March 2022. Not only do they originate from or practice in these two continents, they also belong to different generations, from scholars such as Adrian Forty and Penny Sparke, who initiated their careers collaborating with the British critic and historian back in the 1970s, to others such as Curt Gambetta and Mimi Zeiger who have more recently engaged in different capacities with Banham's work.

    In the spirit of Banham's voracious curiosity and encyclopaedic knowledge, the contributors to this anthology have engaged with a diverse set of topics, from obituaries to sheriff badges, from highly infrastructured urban environments to rarefied desertic landscapes. Not only have they analysed Banham's teaching and research practice, they have also dissected some key chapters from notorious publications such as *Los Angeles: The Architecture* of *Four Ecologies* and *Scenes in America Deserta*. The contributors selected passages and chapters that reflected on the contemporary roles of designers and historians as well as on the practice of fieldwork, and that deeply resonate with enduring and pressing issues such as racial segregation, highlighting passages that remained unresolved or problematic. The tone of the introductory texts are as diverse as Banham's chosen subjects, reflecting the contributors' biographies and relation to Banham: from sharp critical readings to more intimate notes, such as those penned by Tim Street-Porter and Adrian Forty.

This book, which follows two previous anthologies of Banham texts, Whiteley's intellectual biography, Todd Gannon's publication and which arrives shortly after Richard J Williams' biography, aims to shed new light on the British critic and historian's intellectual legacy.[8] The contributors bring to the surface facts and ideas that have eluded historical understanding, as a means to read and test their timeliness in light of our present and future epochal challenges.

1 Reyner Banham, 'The Wilderness Years of Frank Lloyd Wright', in *A Critic Writes: Essays by Reyner Banham*, edited by Mary Banham et al (University of California Press, 1996), pp 137–48.
2 Reyner Banham, 'Actual Monuments', in *A Critic Writes*, pp 281–91.
3 Ibid, p 283.
4 Getty Research Institute, Los Angeles (910009), Ocatillo Project, 1980–83; B.12, F.7.
5 Ludovico Centis, 'Reconstructed Authorship: Wright, Banham and the Ashes of Ocatillo Camp', in *OASE* 113, 2022, pp 45–54.
6 This book emerged from the 1932 exhibition *Modern Architecture: International Exhibition*, held at the Museum of Modern Art in New York and curated by Hitchcock with Philip Johnson.
7 Reyner Banham, 'Actual Monuments', p 291.
8 See respectively Reyner Banham, *Design by Choice*, edited by Penny Sparke (Rizzoli, 1981) and Reyner Banham, *A Critic Writes*; Nigel Whiteley, *Reyner Banham: Historian of the Immediate Future* (MIT Press, 2002); Todd Gannon, *Reyner Banham and the Paradoxes of High Tech* (Getty Trust Publications, 2017); Richard J Williams, *Reyner Banham Revisited* (Reaktion Books, 2021).

Barbara Penner
Mies in the Lavatory

//

Reyner Banham
The Last Professional

Published in *New Society*, 18 December 1969, pp 986–7.

Barbara Penner
Mies in the Lavatory

It is classic Banham. Would anyone else open an obituary by confessing their final encounter with its subject had occurred in the loo? Banham admits some embarrassment, but doesn't hesitate to detail his last interaction with Mies van der Rohe: the door swings open, revealing the architect's 'elaborately wrinkled face' and 'chromium and black leather wheelchair'. Banham says, 'I held the door and said goodbye again – for the last time.'

This paragraph – indeed, the whole obituary – encapsulates the Banhamite method. Banham's admiration for Mies is real, but to approach him seriously, he first has to cut through the aura around him. So he places the 'master', the last *Baukünstler*, in his office toilet in Chicago. We see him as Banham intends: not as a deified figure from the mists of time, but a flesh-and-bone architect at work in his adopted home town. Banham even gives us the address – twice.

For Banham, Mies' context is significant, if underappreciated by the other 'public mouths'. (Banham can never resist a jab at them.) He attributes the 'triumph' of Mies not to Europe but to America. And not to the elite East Coast either, but to the crass commercialism of the Midwest – a point he emphasises by equating Mies' professionalism to that of Hugh Hefner, whose own office was located next door. He quotes Mies on Chicago: 'Here it is a jungle, but at least you can do something.'

This is the key to understanding Mies, Banham tells us. It was never platonic idealism that drove him; it was *doing* – building, and building well. He was devoted to details and to the German craft of construction. After all, even if Mies was 'made' in

America, he was formed in Europe. Banham dashes us nimbly through this lineage: *Playboy* gives way to Paul Valéry's *Eupalinos, ou l'Architecte*, Chicago to the neoclassical Berlin of Schinkel. Mies bridges traditional building practices and the more ineffable *Bildung*; Banham regards his final work, the Berlin Museum (now Neue Nationalgalerie), as the apotheosis of this particularly German cocktail.

The article covers a dazzling amount of ground. Starting as we did, mundanely, in the toilet, we don't expect to end transcendently with a monument. And not just any monument, but what Banham describes as the perfect *Mal* (shortened from *Denkmal*, German for monument). But this act of transcendence is what Banham regards as Mies' unique achievement: the way his painstaking mix of pragmatism, craft and classical culture always ends in work of certitude and rightness.

It is this rightness that plagues the angsty 'Guevaristas' who Banham teases throughout – the younger generation of architects spouting Marcuse and desperate to free architecture from capitalism. They want to dismiss Mies for his commercialism and his lack of a social agenda. Their problem, says Banham, is that they can't deny that Mies is an *architect*, doing architecture as it's been done for as long as there has been architecture. Banham gleefully reports how one of his radical students at The Bartlett is baffled and ultimately defeated by Mies' work, admitting at last, 'It's great architecture!'

Yet the 3,000-year-old tradition that Mies embodies is just as much a problem for Banham as it was for his activist students. As much as he pokes fun at their views – he shows far less sympathy for student protesters than other *New Society* contributors – nobody is more in tune with the larger changes that spawned them. Banham lists them: 'the environmental demands of space travel [...], the ghetto, of tourism, of the automobile, of the Third World, of the youth explosion, of the whole electronic global green spaceship village bit...'

Distancing himself from student activists, while still claiming to speak for the contemporary, requires Banham do some skillful manoeuvering. His solution is to celebrate Mies, but to treat him as the last of his kind, 'the last professional'. His article is thus a dual obituary of Mies and of the 'grand old constructive tradition'. The Berlin Museum becomes a 'terminal monument', a mausoleum for a man whose architectural rightness is no longer right for the times.

It is a respectful burial. But if Banham hoped that, by issuing this death certificate on his own terms, he would retake ground from theory-mad radical students such as Charles Jencks, he was mistaken. The death of the 'neatly assembled certitudes' Mies represents could hardly fail to affect Banham's fixed techno-optimism either. Beneath Banham's trademark jauntiness, we detect a jittery edge, as he faces the unpredictable post-Miesian galaxy.

REYNER BANHAM
THE LAST PROFESSIONAL

There was this architectural detail: a five-inch-square slot running between the top of the wall and the capstone above, all round the 100-metre-square podium on which the building stood. By standing on a snow-covered pile of builders' rubbish, you could look down the slot. It ran absolutely straight and level and in flawless perspective, and only one architect in the world could have demanded it of his builders: old Mies, the last *Baukünstler*. The building was his museum in Berlin, and thereby hangs much irony.

But why am I re-burying Ludwig Mies van der Rohe (born Aachen, 1886; died, Chicago, 1969), a clear four months after the other public mouths have made their obsequies? Simply that he was the only one of the Master generation of modern architects with whom I felt personally involved. The death left me too numb to write – and too, well, embarrassed. I mean, could one *really* begin an obituary with: 'The last time I saw Mies van der Rohe was in the men's lavatory of his office in Chicago...'

It's true, though. I had been in for coffee and chat. The legend of Mies' silence was a myth; he *enjoyed* talking, and treated you as a person, not (like Le Corbusier) as an audience. Afterwards, I was just drying my hands when the lavatory door swung open and there was the unmistakable father-figure, grinning all over his elaborately wrinkled face, in the famous chromium and black-leather wheelchair that had become his normal mode of office locomotion. So I held the door and said goodbye again – for the last time.

That office occupied a whole upper floor of a vaguely thirtyish block on East Ohio Street, a big space with windows all round, filled with drawing boards and architectural models. His own room was in one corner by the elevator; the far end had been partitioned off to form the model-making shop. By a coincidence that one felt must somehow be significant, the windows of the model shop looked across a narrow alley into the windows of what might be called the model shop of the old *Playboy* offices. Architectural model-making became very popular if Hugh Hefner's art-department forgot to draw the curtains on a photographic session.

If not significant, this juxtaposition of Mies and Hefner in Chicago is not ludicrous either. Both, in their own fields, were real, solid, trained-in-the-bone professionals, and Chicago is one of the world's greatest cities – shrines, even – of the culture of professionalism. As Mies said in 1964, judiciously reappraising Chicago after his first trip back to Germany since 1937: 'Here it is a jungle, but at least you can do something.' And he could say that, even though his disgraceful sacking from Illinois Institute of Technology still rankled. He could operate in Chicago as a professional offering an expert service to a commercial community.

    The professionalism in a commercial context needs to be emphasised. So much has been written (largely European wishfulfilment) to make Mies van der Rohe out as a detached aesthete pursuing a platonic ideal of abstract, immaterial space-sculptures, philosopher of 'less is more' and 'almost nothing,' quoter of Aquinas and Augustine in the original tongue, and all the rest of it, that there is still a salutary and refreshing shock in being reminded that he was purveying a saleable product in a buyers' market. The triumph of Mies, his style (and his imitators) came in that most professional period of American history, the grey-flannel years of the Eisenhower regime, and his significant patrons have always tended to be the apparatchiks of the US power-elite, or the entrepreneurs who build for them.

    This puts the architectural commentators of the activist generation in a cleft stick. Even a senior critic like Philip Johnson, who had been Mies's partner in designing the Seagram Building, was referring to his former idol as 'a great conservative' by the early sixties. Younger voices have been harsher, calling him a 'compromiser with a corrupt society,' resurrecting ancient worries about his relations with the Nazis in the thirties. It is a cause of understandable concern to radicals that Mies's architecture implies no pretence to a reform of society (as does that of Gropius, Le Corbusier, Buckminster Fuller). Mies could stand pat on such outrageous statements as: 'The floor-heights are fixed by the building codes, the spans between columns by the financiers.' And if that is a two-dimensional proposition in architecture, it is also bound to sound pretty one-dimensional downstream from Marcuse.

Not that the first wave of academic *Angst* about Mies waited for Marcuse. Early in the sixties I remember standing between the towers of Mies's housing development at Lafayette Park, Detroit, with most of the more vocal members of the Association of Collegiate Schools of Architecture ... and were they having a bitch-in! The end of architecture; computerised inhumanity; slums in the name of technology; 1984; *trahison des clercs* ... you name it, they alleged it.

But the note was to start changing very soon after. In Vincent Scully's *American Architecture and Urbanism*, just published over here (Thames & Hudson, £5.5s) but written in 1966–67, the line on Mies is far gentler than would have seemed conceivable three or four years earlier. Indeed he is seen as embodying some highly acceptable virtues: 'During the early 1950s, the work of Mies did seem to many architects to be the answer to their problem. And it was exactly the kind of answer that Americans instinctively liked, whether they admitted so or not. It was simplified, pure, clean, generalised, reasonable, abstract: the colonial house all over again. Like that house it also involved a framed structure, now the ideal fleshless skeleton of ringing steel.'

Scully, however, is simply seeing as virtues much of what others of his generation denounced as grievous faults. The Guevarista generation's problems, however, stem from the fact they have no doubt that they are faults, but cannot accept that those faults wipe out Mies as an architect. They cannot deny him the right, as a creative spirit, to do his own thing. Nor can they deny that this is also the fundamental thing that architecture has been about, for as long as there has been architecture.

Like Mies himself, but more paradoxically, architectural protest in the US (and every-English-speaking-where else) has a powerfully conservative motivation. Alarmed at a built world of increasing anonymity, interchangeability, expendability and unreasoning universality, architects plump for the unique, permanent and monumental, the old-friend of a building that is recognisably there when you need it. In other words, architecture in the traditional sense. And however much the imitators of Mies may have done to exemplify faceless ubiquity (Castrol House, Euston Centre, Sheffield University, *et*-yawn-*cetera* down your high street and mine), Mies still

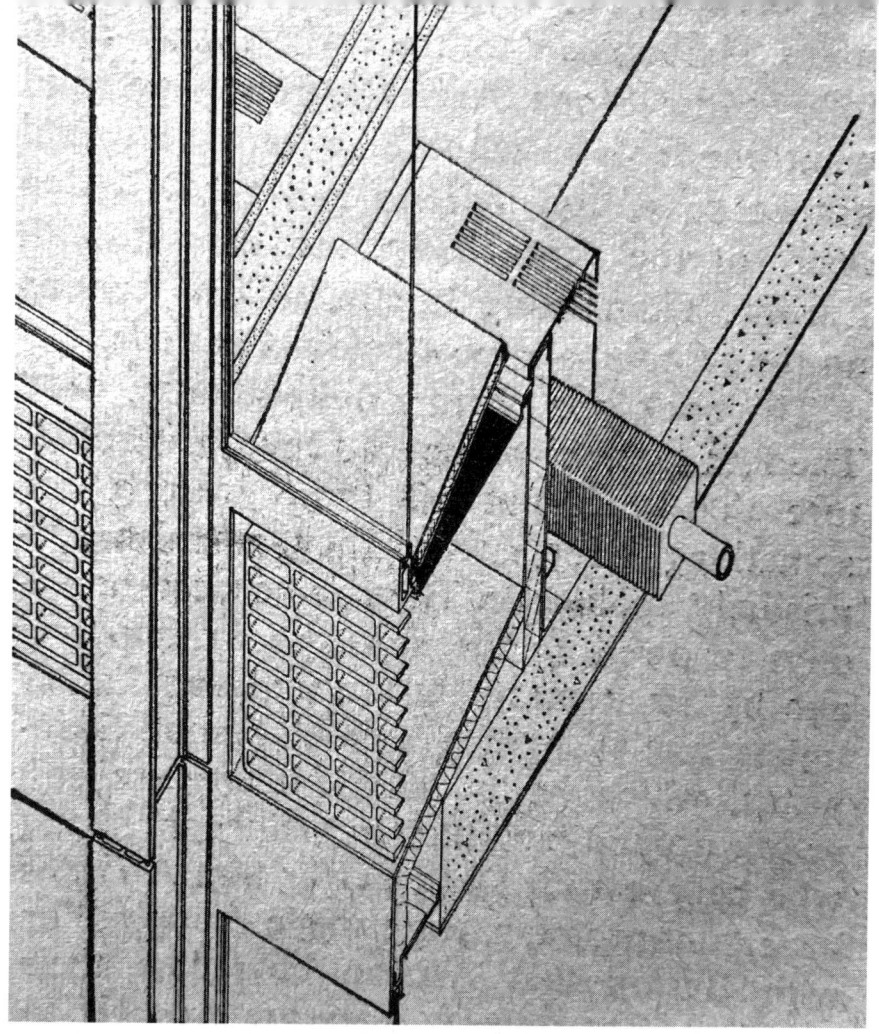
Mies office section of assembled wall, Lafayette Park.

has strong claims as the most fundamental traditionalist of them all. 'It's great architecture!' says one of my more radical students, baffled. (He's the one who thinks the pseudo-Mies architecture of the US Air Force Academy actually *causes* cadets to cheat in their exams.)

To anyone raised in the highly specific subculture of the architectural profession, Mies's architecture is the exercise of the most inward and reverend rituals of the cult. 'How else can we make architecture, but from the means of construction?' asked the old *Baukünstler*; and if you believe that architecture is the art of building well that closes the argument. His buildings are visibly made of nothing but the means of construction: steel, framing glass or brick, and the necessary flanges and flashings to effect the joints between one and the other.

'God is in the details.' Equally, he could have said: 'Architecture is in the joints.' Coming to Chicago from England, where buildings are lumped together from bricks, or Los Angeles where they are smeared into continuous stuccoed surfaces, you are struck again by the way Mies's buildings are joined together out of clearly separate pieces of the means of construction, each of them valued for its unique material qualities: the steel steely, the glass glassy, the aluminium sections properly complex, the mastic sealant gloppy.

Yet this intensely constructed quality is there even in the drawings the office produced, each as clear and orderly as the instructions for a model kit. Which, of course, it was – every Mies building was a model once in its life; probably several models, to try out different arrangements of the blocks, plus details mocked up to quarter, half, or even full scale. The wheelchair would glide silently down the aisle of drawing boards to the model, which would be scrutinised, appraised, discussed, pondered over. And if it didn't get the nod, six months' work might go down the drain. He would have it right, or nothing.

This painstaking devotion to the craft of construction was Mies's greatness and his limitation. Scrupulous attention to detail, within the limits of available technology; constantly refined skill, focused within a narrow cone of vision; unstinted concentration on the job in hand: this is a pure demonstration of the traditional virtue of the architect, as set forth in all the classic literature down to and including Paul Valéry's

Eupalinos, ou l'Architecte (of which there ought to be a new English edition some time, to remind us what the tradition was about). It is also a model demonstration of the benefits and constraints of professionalism – getting the right answer, but always the predictable answer.

With Mies, however, the predictability was enlightening, not lowering. You came to know his buildings in a specially informed way. When I finally got inside the Berlin Museum for the first time, I was physically visiting the *idea* of the building for the fourth or fifth time, for there had long stood in his office a quarter-scale model of one corner of the museum, big enough to stand up in. The real thing was a triumphant confirmation – like, QED – of a proposition already known and thoroughly understood.

But it was also the triumphant confirmation of Mies's whole career. His last monument was in Germany, after all, and in Berlin, the city that had formed him. His whole approach to design – that just blending of craftsmanship and pragmatism within the matrix of a fundamentally classical culture – is not only something that might recommend him to a US elite as an idealised version of The American Way, but it is also the traditional way that has produced any German architecture worth the name, a way compendiously distilled by the great *Handbücher* of the last century out of building practice and the pedagogical mystique of *Bildung*.

In the profoundly German city of Chicago, Mies gave it a stiff compelling eloquence, but Berlin is where it really comes from. In the Berlin of the great neo-classicists Gilly, Schinkel and the whole clan of Gropius, Mies's museum is the deftest and most effective celebration that tradition ever had. Appropriately, it is the ultimate German *Mal*, or ideal monument, aloof, perfected, elevated above the world.

And here's the ultimate irony: nobody else could do it, even in Berlin. Mies's long exile in Chicago preserved a Berlin tradition that was vanishing at home – much as the Elgin marbles in the British Museum are not being weathered into indecipherable oblivion like the carvings that remain in place on the Parthenon. Locally, the profession has taken such a beating from the Nazis, the War, the Peace, the Airlift, the Wall, that none of the survivors would even want to cut a square groove optically straight for a hundred metres. They would rather do something more expressive, but less disconcerting, like Hans Scharoun's Philharmonie, just acros the platz and only four years older, but a galaxy away in its intentions.

But then we are all a galaxy away from the tradition so nobly (not a word I use lightly) embodied by Mies. Justifying themselves, they would say in the office on East Ohio: 'When we build on the moon, maybe we will build like your friend Bucky Fuller...' Well, we're on the moon, and the environmental demands of space travel, coupled with the environmental demands of the ghetto, of tourism, of the automobile, of the Third World, of the youth explosion, of the whole electronic global green space-ship village bit, have called the grand old constructive tradition into question so deeply that its neatly assembled certitude may never stand up to human scrutiny again.

Yet, for the three millenniums of Man's technological infancy it has served us well, and if it had to have a terminal monument it could hardly do better than that soberly arrogant *Mal* in West Berlin, nor could it have had a better and more appropriate last master than exiled Mies van der Rohe. They don't make professionals like that any more.

Penny Sparke
The Dream of Technology

//

Reyner Banham
The Great Gizmo

Published in *Industrial Design*, no 12, September 1965, pp 48–59.

Penny Sparke
The Dream of Technology

Reyner Banham published 'The Great Gizmo' in the US journal *Industrial Design* in September 1965. It represents two of his greatest passions in life: America and technology. Banham has frequently been criticised for putting too much faith in the power of technology to change the world and for aligning himself too strongly with the architectural modern movement. Arguably, though, in 'The Great Gizmo' and other writings such as *The Architecture of the Well-tempered Environment*, he made an important case for its significant role in defining American democracy. In a way, these texts picked up where Sigfried Giedion's influential book *Mechanization Takes Command* – which, published back in 1948, focused on the technological implications of inter-war modernism – left off. Banham took that modernist-inspired text into completely new territory: that of the consumer-dominated post-war world.

Banham was the son of a gas engineer, and before studying to become an architectural historian he was awarded an engineering scholarship by the Bristol Aeroplane Company, for which he worked during much of the Second World War. Engineering and machines were in his blood. He visited the United States from the early 1960s onwards and finally moved there in 1976, teaching first in Buffalo and later in Santa Cruz. However, he had already acquired an extensive body of knowledge about the US in the 1950s through his membership of The Independent Group, a knowledge that derived from the world of popular culture – sci-fi movies, pulp novels, popular magazines etc. For Banham, America was the home of Hollywood films and stylish automobiles.

In 'The Great Gizmo', Banham turns his attention to gizmos, or gadgets (he undoubtedly liked the sound of the words and the alliteration) – among them the Evinrude outboard motor, the cordless shaver, walkie-talkies, air-conditioners and waste disposers. The gizmo, he sets out to demonstrate, had made the US what it was and it was the technological inventiveness of its citizens that had created 'The American Way of Life'. For Banham, new technologies and gadgets gave the American citizen the freedoms and democratic rights that defined their modern existence, although the sense of control that technology offered could, he felt, be an illusory one. Without gizmos, Banham claims, the West would never have been won and the wilderness never tamed. Today, these claims for the civilising benefits of the gizmo can be seen as endorsing the colonial and imperial behaviour of European settlers at the expense of the Indigenous population, but he does not seem to be aware of those implications.

    He also makes a case for Americans loving industry and mechanisation in a way that never happened in the 'Old World'. Above all, and this is why Banham loved America so much: gizmos, in his view, trampled over class differences and promised everyone access to the 'good life'. He even defends Coca-Cola – through an attitude towards 'native culture' which today reads as rather problematic – explaining that, despite the unpleasantness of the capitalist message their dispenser machines carried, they displayed high levels of hygiene wherever they were found around the world.

    The essay exudes a sense of (typically Banhamesque) breathless enthusiasm. It comes straight from the heart and lacks bookishness. With much extravagant language on show – he calls Catherine Beecher 'one of the Founding Dames of the suburban way of life' – Banham extols the role of the gizmo. However, he is also at pains to make a serious academic point, which is that gizmos don't have the 'intellectual support and scrutiny' that they deserve. While this essay cannot be described as a 'general theory of the gizmo' it offers a powerful and emotional appeal for us not to ignore them.

REYNER BANHAM
THE GREAT GIZMO

'The purpose of technology is to make the dream a fact... The end is to make the Earth a garden, Paradise; to make the mountain speak.'

– Arthur Drexler

The man who changed the face of America had a gizmo, a gadget, a gimmick – in his hand, in his back pocket, across the saddle, on his hip, in the trailer, round his neck, on his head, deep in a hardened silo. From the Franklin Stove, and the Stetson Hat, through the Evinrude outboard to the walkie-talkie, the spray can and the cordless shaver, the most typical American way of improving the human situation has been by means of crafty and usually compact little packages, either papered with patent numbers, or bearing their inventor's name to a grateful posterity. Other nations, such as Japan may now be setting a crushingly competitive pace in portable gadgetry, but their prime market is still the US and other Americanised cultures, while America herself is so prone to clasp other cultures' key gadgets to her acquisitive bosom that their original inventors and discoverers are forgotten – 'Big Kahuna' mysticism aside, even the Australians seem to have forgotten that they were the first White Anglo-Saxon Protestants to steal the surfboard from the Polynesians, so thoroughly has surfing been Americanised. So ingrained is the belief in a device like a surfboard as the proper way to make sense of an unorganised situation like a wave, that when Homo Americanus finally sets foot on the moon it will be just as well the gravity is only one sixth of earth's for he is likely to be so hung about with packages, kits, black boxes and waldos that he would have a job to stand under any heavier 'g'.

LANDSCAPE WITH FIGURES WITH GADGETS

True sons of Archimedes, the Americans have gone one better than the old grand-daddy of mechanics. To move the earth he required a lever long enough and somewhere to rest it – a gizmo and an infrastructure – but the great American gizmo can get by without any infrastructure. Had it needed one, it would never have won the West or opened up the transcontinental trails. The quintessential gadgetry of the pioneering frontiersman had to be carried across trackless country, set down in a wild place, and left to transform that hostile environment without skilled attention. Its function was to bring instant order or human comfort into a situation which had previously been an undifferentiated mess, and for this reason it is so deeply involved with the American mythology of the wilderness that its philosophy will bear looking into, both for its American consequences, and for the consequences of its introduction into other landscapes, other scenes.

Underneath lies that basic confusion about the American landscape – is it a wilderness or a paradise? – that has bedevilled American thought from Walden Pond to the barbecue pit in the backyard, a confusion on which Leo Marx's recent book *The Machine in the Garden* is so illuminating on every aspect except industrial design. Marx observes that the early settlers brought with them from Europe 'the pastoral ideal of a rural nation exhibiting a happy balance of art and nature', and continues 'In this sentimental guise the pastoral ideal remained of service long after the machine's appearance in the landscape. It enabled the nation to continue defining its purpose as the pursuit of rural happiness while devoting itself to productivity, wealth and power. It remained for our serious writers to discover the meaning inherent in the contradiction.'

Now, from a less bookish standpoint, it might appear that the contradiction between industry and garden is only a local disturbance – local in time as well as space – in a more widespread process of employing machinery to make the pastoral garden-ideal available to the whole nation. Local in time, because one of the surest ways to convert the American wilderness into the American paradise is to let agronomy or industry pass across it and then vanish – as witness the second growth woodlands of Connecticut that have supplanted a vanished agriculture and produced perhaps the most paradisal suburban landscape in the world (or, again, I know areas in the Middle West where the mere mowing and brush-cutting of an abandoned farm will produce a landscape that could have come from the brush of Claude Lorraine). Local in space because the ground permanently occupied or permanently blighted by US industry is still infinitesimal compared with the vast acreage opened up to human settlement by industry's products.

Portable technology closes Leo Marx's contradiction as surely as do the meanings discovered by serious writers: industrial productivity was perhaps the only means of converting the disorderly wilderness into an humane garden. For, if there is rural happiness in America that is in any way comparable with the European pastoral dream – whether noble, as in Palladio's villas, or ridiculous, as in Marie-Antoinette's spoof dairymaiding – it depends on technology rather than serfdom or chattel-slavery as it did in the Old World. Yes, agreed – the American pastorale probably did start in slave-owning Virginia (though Monticello was full of mechanical ingenuities) but the dream's proliferation beyond the Appalachians, beyond the Mississippi, beyond the Rockies, increasingly depended at every stage upon the products of industry and the local application of mechanisms. For the first time, a civilisation with a flourishing industry encountered a landscape that was entirely virgin or, at worst, inhabited by scattered tribes of noble (or preferably, dead) savages.

In Europe and the Orient, industry has had to worm its ways into the interstices of an already crowded pattern of social strata and landownership: over most of the US there was neither society nor landownership until mechanisation came puffing in on railroads that were often the first and only geographical fixes the Plains afforded. In Europe, the pastoral ideal is the heir of the medieval *hortus clusus* or walled garden – from the landscape parks of the eighteenth century to the nudist colonies of the twentieth, the pastoral dream has meant withdrawal behind protective barriers to keep out the pressure of the hoi polloi. In America the pastoral ideal is available to the hoi polloi as well, and if he wants wilderness the average man rarely has to drive for more than an hour to find unimproved ground – remember, pockets of undisturbed prairie ecology survive even in Gary, Indiana. The pastoral ideal in the USA is an extraverted vision, and while Manhattan-based Jeremiahs moan over the disappearance of the wilderness, Europeans (who really know about intensive occupation of land) goggle unbelievingly still at the empty acres beyond the filling stations and hamburger stands along the freeway.

Japanese Toyota Land Cruiser station wagon and pickup truck.

THE TECHNOLOGIST ON THE BACK PORCH

Rural happiness in the US was never to be the privilege of the few, but was to be the common property of every member of every family, thanks to domestic mechanisation. The good life offered by early visionaries of the railroad-age such as Catherine Beecher, is of enjoyable industry for the entire family, the cultivation of the mind as well as cotton and vegetables; and it already depends, in 1869, on a notable level of mechanical sophistication. As James Marston Fitch pointed out in his key study of the redoubtable Beecher in *Architecture and the Aesthetics of Plenty*, the house she describes in 'The American Woman's Home', is firmly visualised as a true machine for living in, and already boasts such characteristic gadgetry as a pair of Franklin stoves on the main floor and a hot-air stove in the basement, while the domestic economy practised therein with such devoted industry depends, by implication (as Fitch indicates), on equipment such as the Mason jar.

If Catherine Beecher is indeed one of the Founding Dames of the suburban way of life, then the spread of that way of life from coast to coast depended not only on back-porch technologies (to which I shall return in a moment) such as fruit-preserving, but also on one other major factor which is astonishingly missing from most generalised histories of US culture – mail-order shopping. Whatever Messrs Colt and Winchester (two more characteristic gizmo-names) may have done to subdue the West, it was Messrs Sears and Roebuck who made it first habitable and then civilised. Yet their crucial contribution rates no more than the most passing reference, unsupported by discussion or index-reference in Max Lerner's giant coast-to-coast national-economy-sized bromide, *America as a Civilization*. The Sears catalogue is one of the great and basic documents of US civilisation, and deserves the closest critical study wherever the state of the Union is discussed.

One thing the student will observe is that the catalogue rarely fails to quote, along with the price and so forth, the shipping-weight of all mechanical kit. This point has its significance in the history of American technology: where distances were great and transport difficult, costs of freightage could overwhelm the economic value of a low-grade product. Whatever was shipped had to have a high selling price, or social value, relative to its bulk and weight, otherwise it was not worth the trouble. Thus, mill-cut timber was only the base material for the balloon-frame house that sheltered the West – what made it possible to give up building log-cabins was, above all else, the incredibly cheap wire nails that began to come in around the mid-century, and were shipped everywhere in bulk by barrel and bag. Here was a product whose social utility rested upon its cheapness and reliability and vastly outweighed its shipping charges. Furthermore, it was a fixing-device that required general native cunning rather than specific craft skill to employ, and so it came readily to the hand of the householder employing back-porch technologies comparable to those his wife was employing in the kitchen. For this is another key characteristic of the gizmos that changed the face of America: they do not require high skill at the point of application, they leave craftsmanship behind at the factory. Ideally, you peel off the packaging, fix four bolts and press the Go button.

    This is what makes Ole Evinrude's invention of the outboard motor so triumphantly American an event. To fit an inboard motor to an existing boat requires craft skills and mathematical aptitudes of a sort normally found only in places with a long tradition of boat-craft, as in the maritime cities of Europe or New England, where boatyards, shipwrights and the encrusted wisdom of ancient mariners was freely available. But every portage made by the pioneers took them one more river away from any such craft-infrastructure, their boats would normally be the first and only on their particular stretch of water (as are a high proportion of US boats to this day). Their back-porch technologies were unlikely to include either the tackle or the skill to bore a shaft-hole through a keel or transom, fit tube and shaft, make it watertight, calculate (let alone fabricate) the pitch and diameter of propeller, and so forth. But you can order a stock outboard from the catalogue with the right propeller for its own power and your size of boat, fix it with two clamps, add fuel and pull the starter. So ideal, and so American is this solution, that other one-shot aids to the back-porch technologist have proliferated – to cite only one, the adapters that make it possible for any hot-rod-crazy to fit any engine to almost any gearbox and transmission. Warshawsky's current catalogue has three pages of them.

ABSTRACT AND CONSEQUENCES OF THE GIZMO

At this point we have seen enough of the basic proposition, to formulate some generalised rules for the American gizmo, and examine its consequences in design and other fields. Like this: a characteristic class of US products – perhaps the most characteristic – is a small self-contained unit of high performance in relation to its size and cost, whose function is to transform some undifferentiated set of circumstances to a condition nearer human desires. The minimum of skill is required in its installation and use, and it is independent of any physical or social infrastructure beyond that by which it may be ordered from a catalogue and delivered to its prospective user.

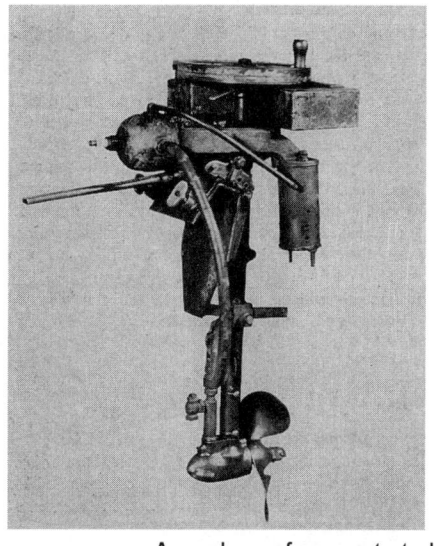

Ole Evinrude's 1909 outboard motor.

As a class of servants to human needs, these clip-on devices, these portable gadgets, have coloured American thought and action far more deeply – I suspect – than is commonly understood. The US tourist hung about with expensive cameras, most of them automated to within an inch of their lives, is a common figure of fun from Jerez to Macao, from Trondheim to Trincomalee, but he is, perhaps, a more tragic figure than a comical one, for it is difficult not to suspect

EF Johnson Company's walkie-talkie.

Remington's cordless shaver.

32   Reyner Banham   A Set of Actual Tracks

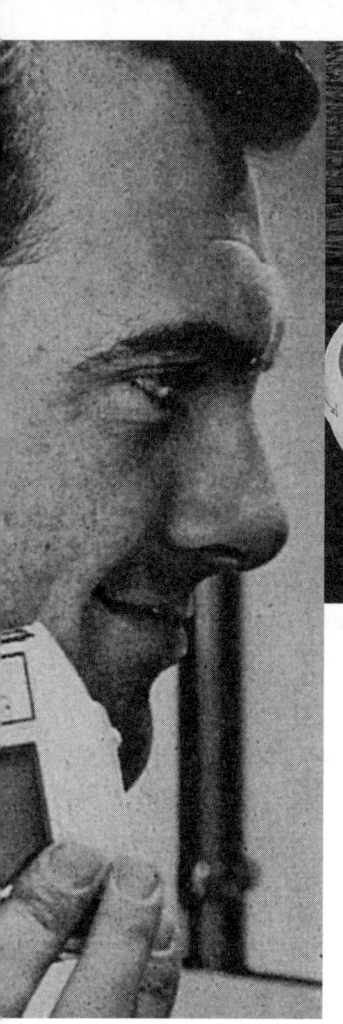

Evinrude powers a Viking Engineering Whirl-O-Bird.

The Great Gizmo

that presented with scenes from cultures that he does not understand he hopes to gizmo them into comprehensible form by pointing the little black box and pressing the trigger. It may not reduce the world to a pastoral, but it will make standardised Kodachrome sense on a screen in the living-room, and it's a lot simpler than learning the language. And if you must learn the language, sitting down at a language-lab will give you a gizmo'd knowledge of the tongue far quicker than walking the streets of Amsterdam trying to strike up conversations in Dutch with passers-by (who always turn out to be Chinese-speaking Indonesians, anyhow).

Because practically every new, incomprehensible or hostile situation encountered by the growing American Nation was conquered, in practice, by handy gizmos of one sort or another, the grown Nation has tended to assume that all hostile situations will be solved with gadgets. If a US ally is in trouble, Uncle Sam rolls up the sleeves of his Arsenal-of-Democracy sweatshirt and starts packing arms in crates for shipment long before he thinks of sending soldiers or diplomats – and be it noted that it was a half-breed American, Winston Churchill, who responded in terms that were pure gizmo-culture; 'Give us the tools and we'll finish the job!' Current US foreign policy, Rand Corporation/Strangelove style, revolves disproportionately (it might be argued) around king-sized gadgets whose ballistic complexity and sheer tonnage should not blind us to the fact that they are still kissin'-cousins to Colt and Winchester, and that the abstract concept of weaponry is simply Sears' catalogue re-written in blood and radiation-sickness. And, now that internal subversion has joined the ranks of 'thinkable' topics in Vietnam and Santo Domingo (not to mention Harlem and Georgia) don't the departments of State and Interior wish there existed some opinion-forming gizmo (guts by IBM and RCA, box-work by Eliot Noyes, graphics by Paul Rand) that could be parachuted down, untouched by human hand, to spread sweetness and light and democracy and free-enterprise for fifty miles around ground-zero. It would beat ugly Americans any day.

It might work, at that – remember how the transistor radios that have replaced Field-Marshals' batons in every *poilu's* knapsack helped De Gaulle rally wavering troops in the last agonies of the Algerian crisis. But there are many situations that can't be resolved by gadgetry, however inspired, and the general reliance of the US on gizmo solutions (helicopters in Viet Nam, recoil-less rifles in Dominica) appears to Old World observers to have landed America in more messes than it has cleared up. This is not to say that Old World methods such as back-stage arm-twisting or political blackmail would have done any better. It is just that gadgetry is unfamiliar to Old World diplomats and is an easy target for blame.

An Army helicopter in Viet Nam.

Unfortunately, gadgetry is also unfamiliar to many of those entrusted with the formation of higher opinion and the direction of academic study in the US, and loses thereby the kind of intellectual support and scrutiny it deserves if it is to produce its promised benefits in the changed circumstances of today. I have already cited one failure of Max Lerner; let me cite another and then leave him be. In positively the worst chapter of *America as a Civilization*, that on architecture and design, he claims that the US has failed to produce a great domestic architecture, because:

'Great architecture is based on belief. Americans have not yet developed a way of domestic life sharply enough differentiated so that a system of belief can be built on it, and in turn give rise to a distinctive architecture. But they do believe in their system of technology. To put it differently, Americans have had greater success with the arts of consumption and comfortable living than with the problem of their life purposes. Wherever they have built structures connected with production ... there has been a sureness about them absent from the recent fumblings with domestic architecture.'

Two Jeeps.

Polaroid Land camera.

There, if ever, was a man with his finger on the Go button but didn't know it. Even at the time he was writing (1956–7) the under-window air-conditioner and the under-sink waste-disposer had differentiated US domestic architecture from all preceding domestic architectures and introduced new freedoms in design that the pioneer Modern architects never enjoyed, while the consequences have more to say about the life-purposes of most Americans than all the University humanities programmes joined end-to-end. Americans believe in technology and that is where to look for the greatness of their domestic architecture – as every envious housewife of Europe, Asia and South America could tell you. In the process, the structure of the US house becomes little more than an undifferentiated shell within which the gizmos can do their work, and its external form acquires a slightly improvised quality, an indecisive shape. But this is not necessarily to be brushed off as fumbling – it may be necessary experimentation or temporising until a definitive shape (or some convincing solution of a nonformal kind) emerges to fix the style of the gizmo-residence – experiments like Harry Weese's row-houses in Old Town, Chicago, where the air-conditioners have been built into cupboard-backs that are the least permanent, most easily altered, parts of the structure.

Instances of failures to comprehend the extent and potential of gadget culture are all too easy to multiply, but my concern here is more with the results of this lack of intellectual grip. One outstanding example is the failure to question the present dwindling independence of the gizmo, its increasing reliance upon an infrastructure it could once do without. While the walkie-talkie has cut men free of networks and wiring, the outboard motor persistently grows in sophistication and dependence – it has acquired a dash-mounted control panel and control lines, a steering harness and wheel, external fuel tank and pipe-runs and, occasionally, external electrics as well. As it becomes more integrated with the boat structure at large, it doubtless acquires something of that mystical 'unity' that Old World pundits and New World academics believe to be the essence of 'a good design', but as it passes out of the capabilities of the back-porch technologist and into the hands of the skilled shipwright, its social usefulness is severely qualified. Again, while Dr Land's Polaroid camera is finally extricating photography from the Victorian impedimenta that has lumbered it since the time of Daguerre, Detroit is producing increasingly limp-wristed automobiles that find it harder and harder to function away from the smooth concrete of the freeway. I don't wish to sound like William Buckley calling for a return to the hairy virtues of the frontier at a time when increasing affluence and improved social techniques make more expensive and interdependent solutions possible, but there are one or two counts on which these present developments might be held up for closer examination.

WILDERNESS IN SEARCH OF GIZMOS

One such count is foreign aid: many of the development countries, especially in Africa, are in a condition sufficiently analogous to that of the West in the early Sears Roebuck epoch, for American experience to have directly useful relevance. Instead, such countries find themselves being bullied into sinking aid funds in massive infrastructure of a kind the US got along without for several generations, whereas small sophisticated devices that can work without much capital investment under them might produce better immediate results and leave the ground free for even more sophisticated developments in these countries later on. Many Africans are disappointed and suspicious about this US attitude which they regard as the extension of Anglo-French colonialism by other means. In particular they suspect that the aim is to create road surfaces on which the current Detroit product will look less ridiculous than it does on the dirt roads over which Soviet and East German vehicles can bump along regardless, and the other thing they suspect is that the money is being directed into heavy investment in order to keep it out of consumer goods industries that might compete directly with the US. One African I know rolled it all up neatly into a big ball of dung by saying 'If the money was ours to spend without Washington's "advice" we would build a factory to manufacture the Japanese Toyota, which retains all the virtues which the Jeep has lost.'

The Jeep makers could doubtless rebut this statement till they were blue in the face, but the fact remains that the Jeep image has lost its ruggedness, has ceased to hold the reputation of a pioneer (and not only in Africa, to judge from the number of Toyotas one seems to see in the mountain states of the US). And there are also some hesitancies, among those who administer or influence aid, that make them unwilling to introduce the independent US gizmo in undeveloped lands; chiefly, a certain squeamishness about introducing familiar brand-names into territories where they might be regarded as dollar imperialism. There is, for instance, a distinct visual and cultural shock in suddenly coming on a Coca-Cola dispenser in Latin America or the Arab States, it is apt to look like a visitor from Mars even in the more rural or desert parts of the USA. It has an almost surreal independence of its rough surroundings as it sits snug in its stylists' chrome and enamel, compact, selfcontained – an alien. To many sensitive souls it is an offense that they would rather not see perpetrated; and it also implies a criticism of its surroundings.

For whatever unpleasant capitalist habits of mind it may exemplify, it always, in such surroundings, guarantees a higher level of hygiene and technique than the native culture affords. Coke is not a product that can be dispensed through a system of hollow reeds and dried gourds supported in a structure made of adobe blocks, any more than there was ever a wood-burning outboard motor. It imports into surroundings that are – for worse or better – less highly-developed, a standard of technical performance that the existing culture of those surroundings could no more support unaided than could the Arkansas territory when it was first purchased. Unfortunately, much of what has just been said is equally true of Coke machines that stand in some of America's older cities, and this brings up another point about the present crisis of the gizmo that is worth discussing here.

THE CITY AS PRE-GIZMOS ARCHAEOLOGY

North America's cities of pre-Industrial foundation – Montreal, Boston, New York, Philadelphia through to New Orleans – could be regarded as the archaeological remains of a culture that ought to have died when the gizmos came in. They represent the kind of enormously massive infrastructural deposits that are left behind by handicraft civilisations, for (in the absence of rapid communications and compact artificial power-sources) the only way to get anything even half-way clever done was to pile men up in vast unhygienic heaps (and anyone who has seen the recently published sootfall statistics for East Side Manhattan will know that they are still unhygienic today). On such man-warrens were built the only concepts of civilisation that we know, but this does not mean that alternative structures of civilisation are not possible, and on this basis the culture of the gizmo, with its accompanying catalogue and distribution network, will bear looking into.

And it is being looked into, at this very moment, by every egg-head who claims a 'discriminating attitude toward the mass media'. In, say, Chicago, he consults the catalogue (radio programmes in the *Daily News*) presses the Go button of his gizmo (AM/FM transistor portable) and connects himself to the distribution net (WFMT your fine art programme) for the *Well-Tempered Clavier*. The distributive civilisation of gizmo culture is here already – and if that does not sound a very original observation thirty years after Frank Lloyd Wright's injunction to 'Watch the little gas station' let me rephrase his accompanying deduction that cities are outmoded in a different key. If the nation is to continue defining its purpose

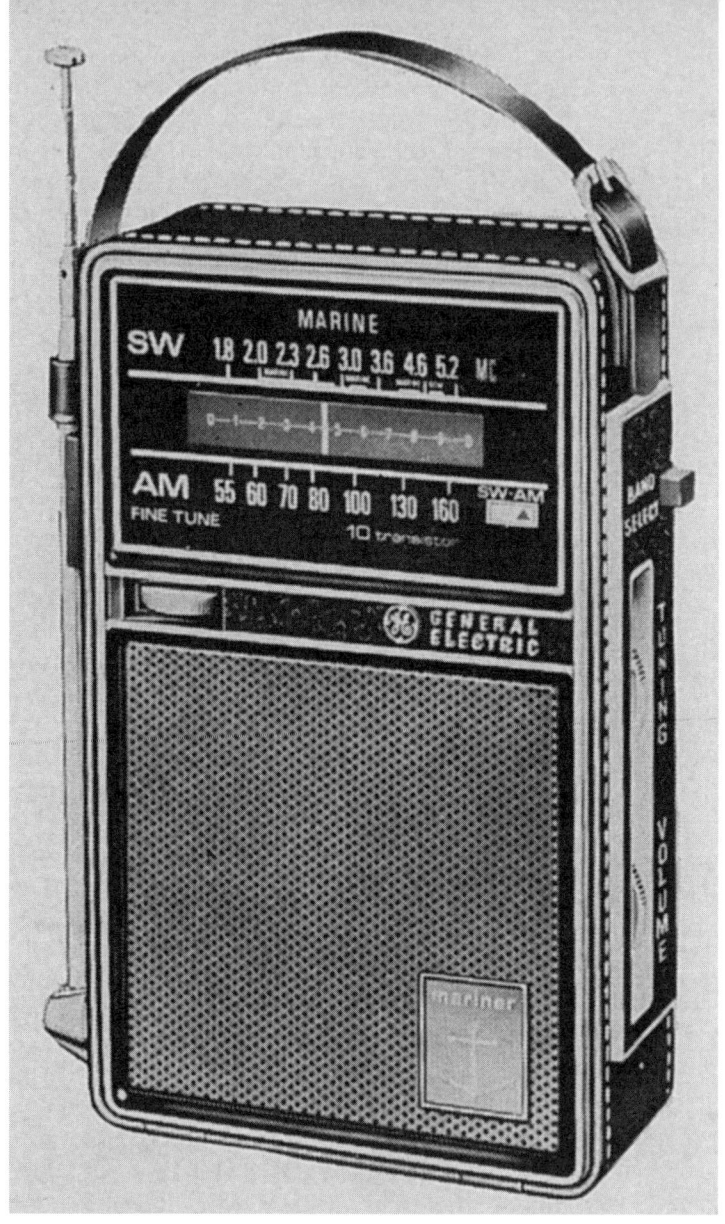

General Electric's Mariner transistor radio.

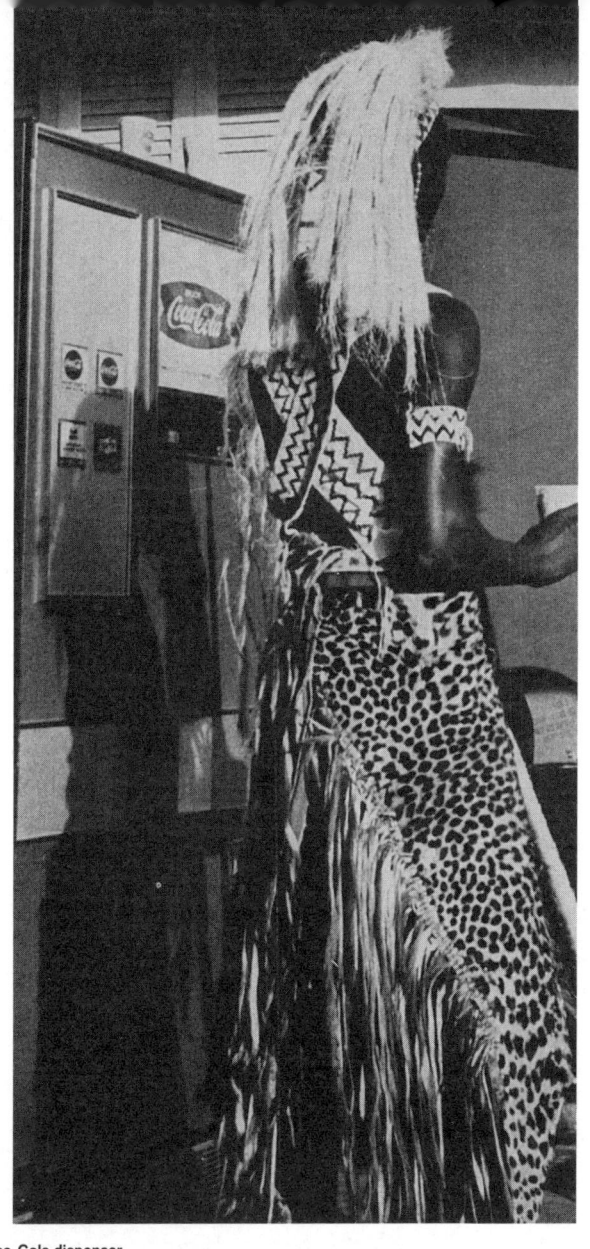

The ubiquitous Coca-Cola dispenser.

The Great Gizmo

as the pursuit of rural happiness, and if its population is to continue expanding at the present rate, then it may soon become necessary to re-suburbanise existing urban sites and to reduce them to quasi-rural population densities. You have only to go up to the Cloisters or Fort Tryon and look around you, to realise that Manhattan Island would be the most paradisal of American Gardens if only they would get New York off it. So I exaggerate? But not very much; there are many semi-urban areas – the centre of Denver, Colorado, for instance – that could still be rearranged to both their immediate and future advantage provided they do not get buried any deeper than at present, in old-fashioned urban infrastructure. The future, at a modest guess, is going to require a much more flexible distribution of American citizens on the ground, and this is going to be much easier to effect if they can pick up their culture and ride than if they are pinned to the ground by vast masses of Lincoln Centre style masonry.

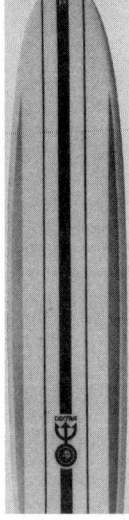

Accurate System's surfboard.

The traditional American wooden house has always sat lightly on its terrain – a smart hurricane or runaway Mack truck will remove it neatly, leaving just 12 posts and 2 pipes sticking out of the lawn. This potentiality seems to trouble architects to the bottoms of their monumental souls, but it has always fascinated US technologues, from Bucky Fuller's Dymaxion houses to the Clark Cortez campers that suddenly seem to be the queens of the American road. Indeed, a self-propelled residential gizmo seems to be a kind of ultimate in the present state of US culture. The Clark's running gear is a hot-rodder compilation of proprietary catalogue components, and once tanked up and its larder stocked it is independent of all infrastructures for considerable periods of time – it need not deposit sewage or waste every time it comes to an overnight halt, so that when it moves off again the next morning, and the grass that was pressed down by its wheels has recovered its normal habit, that piece of the face of America remains as unchanged as if four persons and a package of sophisticated technology had never been there. A piece of the American wilderness had been, briefly, a piece of the American Paradise-garden, and could then return to wild.

NAME IT, THEN WE'LL KNOW WHAT IT IS

No doubt this vision of a gas-powered pastorale, a great nation pursuing rural happiness down the highway, is oversimplified, but observe that it has at its heart a discrete and factual object. The Cortez exists already and can be bought ex-catalogue and increasing numbers of Americans will buy them because the most fundamental American response to dreams is to purchase a piece of equipment to make them come true. And dreams aside, the facts about the Cortez are that its residential performance is considerably superior to that of the handsome Jane Jacobs-type brownstone in which I am writing these words, and its mobility is far superior to that of even the most sophisticated trailers because it is just one single compact unit running on only four wheels. For design people at the Aspen Conference this year to respond to the Clark Cortez only with complaints about its colour-scheme or 'It's an ugly brute,' seems a pitifully inadequate response to what may be one of the most portentous events in the history of the North American continent.

Maybe portentous, or maybe not – but in the absence of a general theory of the gizmo by which to evaluate it, we do not know. The number of breaks in the wall of academic ignorance mentioned earlier has been small indeed, even in the twenty years or so since Sigfried Giedion first tickled the topic in *Mechanization Takes Command*. The subject still lacks a radical theorist who will range freely over departmental barriers and disciplinary interfaces and come back with a comprehensive historical account of the rise of portable gadgetry, and deduce from it some informed projections of the good or evil future it affords.

Perhaps his first task might be to think of a better name for his topic than 'Gizmology', but it may be difficult. The original impetus to write this article came from the impact of a single very precise and concrete image – a man carrying a portable welding plant across the Utah salt-flats with one hand – and the impact of this image was extremely specific. Not 'This man is carrying a portable gadget of typically US format,' but 'This man is carrying a welding plant'. The whole gizmo bit revolves around such unique and discrete objects, named after the specific functions they serve, and this indeed is the prime utility of the whole approach: whatever you want to do, the precise gadget is in the catalogue. But because the whole bit is made up of these genuinely independent parts, each as private and aloof as the Coke dispenser in the Casbah, it remains extremely difficult to generalise about them, even to find them a generic name which will, after they have been a hundred years in the field, acknowledge their nation-wide importance on the changed face of America.

Mario Carpo
From Softer Hardware to Software

//

Reyner Banham
Softer Hardware

Published in *ARK – Journal of the Royal College of Art*, no 44, 1969, pp 2–11.

Mario Carpo
From Softer Hardware to Software

In the summer of 1969, industrial modernity was in trouble. It was not running out of oil or raw materials – that will come a bit later. It was running out of favour. In 1921 Le Corbusier thought that mass-produced automobiles were the future, and that future, seen from 1921, looked promising. In 1969 that future has come, and Banham finds it 'boring'.

Mass production achieves economies of scale through product standardisation, but, as Banham acknowledges in 1969, successful standardised products, when they end up being everywhere, look bland and lose all charm. Therefore, Banham claims, 'post-industrial societies' must find ways to bring back some form of 'variability' and 'surprise' into mass production; Banham's solution, his alternative to the standard car is the 'customised car', a car that must be 'as unique as its maker'. But mind Banham's words: as its maker – not as its owner.

The car industry itself had already started to market customisable cars via catalogue-based, multiple choice options. But Banham had another model in mind: activist, hands-on customisation, as practiced by the hot-rodder movement. Hot-rodders are car enthusiasts who modify and retrofit standard cars, through ad-hoc improvements but mostly using ready made parts, bought and sold on secondary markets. The movement exists to this day but it was big in the 1960s. The hot-rodders were early hackers – they did not buy a customised car; they bought a standard car, then they customised it.

By arguing for customisation, differentiation, variation and choice Banham was in fact foreshadowing some core principles of what today we call postmodernism. Nor was he the only one, in 1969, to feel that the culture of standardisation had run its course. *Complexity and Contradiction in Architecture* had been published in 1966. And in 1964 Marshall McLuhan had already suggested quite a different technical fix for the same problem: a new kind of computer-driven assembly line, McLuhan claimed, will soon start to mass produce customised pieces instead of standard ones; computer-driven electronic machines can manufacture 80 different kinds of automobile tailpipes at the same price as 80 identical ones.[1]

This is what today we call digital mass customisation; computer-controlled milling machines of the type that McLuhan seemed to have in mind had been tested at MIT since 1959, but back then there was no name – and no market – for computer-driven mass customisation. McLuhan singularly expanded on the same topic in other writings of the late 1960s, but at the time nobody noticed. Nor did Banham.

For Banham at the time showed little affection for the incipient and rising tools of 'computerisation'. He saw computers primarily as means of electronic control, invisible snoops which inspire 'worry' and 'alarm', to be 'diverted and disrupted' by hippies and saboteurs. All electronic networks, in Banham's view, are 'hardware'; the only possible software is human creativity – hence Banham's plea, and the title of the piece. Banham did not care about electronics. Even when anticipating activist hacking and crowdsourcing, Banham celebrates the power and the glory of the mechanical age. McLuhan's future was made of bits and bytes; Banham's, of nuts and bolts.

History has already disproven Banham's prophecy. Today we know that the answer to the cultural decline of high modernism, and to the technological obsolescence of the first machine age, would not come from taming and tweaking the assembly line – from making 'softer hardware', as Banham thought in 1969. It would come from software. But Banham, who died in 1988, would not live to see that.

1   Marshall McLuhan, *Understanding Media: The Extension of Man* (McGraw-Hill, 1964), p 314.

REYNER BANHAM
SOFTER HARDWARE

Design thinking, design teaching, and design practice are still largely in the thrall of the factory system mythology. The context in which most designers see their tasks (especially when they think they are being hard nosed and realistic) is the context of raw materials being taken to large centralised plants where they are converted into inanimate objects which are then distributed from the central plant. The human race only enters this system at two points – by going to the factory to participate in the process of production, and by standing at the end of the process as the ultimate consumer.

This factory system, from Arkwright's spinning jenny to Henry Ford's taylorised production line, was conceived in terms of the clear separation of productive and consumptive functions and clearly separate productive and consumptive roles on the part of human beings. It may be that this distinction was the product of the dehumanising and alienating philosophy implied in the concept of a division of labour, but it may equally come from the physical make up of the machinery involved – it was too big to have in the home; it made too hostile an environment to live in.

It's all very well for Karl Marx and his followers to come on moralistic about the alienation of the worker from the means of production, but I doubt if anything else was physically possible in the first stages of mechanised production of goods. The upshot was that by the end of the nineteenth century, all but the most primitive and ancient technologies, such as cookery, had vanished from the domestic experience of western man.

Especially the domestic experience of western intellectuals. It is worth remembering that the design moralities of men like Ruskin and Morris were elaborated in almost total lack of experience of what factory production was like in physical fact; neither shows much awareness of the psychological rewards of working with machinery, only the deprivations. It was left to a later generation – the Futurists in the nineteen teens and the abstract artists of the nineteen twenties to point out that machinery alone could save men's lives being blighted by the slavery of repetitious handicraft. 'Under the supremacy of materialism,' wrote van

Doesburg, 'handicraft reduced men to the level of machines; the proper tendency for the machines is as the unique medium of social liberation. Every machine represents the spiritualisation of an organism.'

Van Doesburg and his abstract art cronies in the early twenties could say this, were forced to say it almost, because they had observed at close range, and from the relatively low eye level of children, the entry of mechanisms into the home. They were the first generation whose floor games were disturbed not by the broom but by the vacuum cleaner, the first generation whose mothers arranged their social round by telephone and whose entertainment was not sweated out by hand at the piano but delivered in neat plastic cylinders courtesy of Thomas Alva Edison. Theirs was the generation whose maidservants had been socially liberated from half their worst housework and laundering chores by the new clean electric light. Their unique historical experience is summed up in one of the drawings in Osbert Lancaster's *Homes Sweet Homes* – an Edwardian interior with electric light on the ceiling, a telephone on the wall and a small boy in a sailor suit standing on the bound works of HG Wells to listen to a His-Master's-Dog-type gramophone.

Yet, in spite of these experiences, so powerful has been the thrall of the factory system mythology that we have almost entirely failed to follow up those shrewd perceptions of the early twenties. We have praised the Bauhaus for designing light fittings that show complete alienation from the human user. Praised them for being cheap and simple to produce in the factory – but failed to damn them for producing intolerable glare in the home of the consumer. It is not a change of fashion that has relegated some of the Bauhaus style light fittings to remand homes, fish and chip shops, and church halls, it is their basically unfunctional character in the human context. And the lamp fittings that have thankfully driven out the well intentioned Bauhaus rubbish have all come from areas that were not in thrall – economically or culturally – to the factory system.

They were designed by people like Kaare Klint in Scandinavia and Jørn Utzon, by Gio Ponti in Italy and by Carlo Mollino. But many of the best came from people like George Nelson and all those prize winners in the Heifetz lamp competition of

1960 – the Charles Eames generation in the USA. The Scandinavians and the Italians had largely missed the full horrors and alienations of the monumental phase of the factory system and had never needed to get so screwed up about it as the French, Germans, Belgians and Anglo-Saxons. But the Americans had already sweated through the factory system phase and had come out the other side into what is now called post-industrial society. For them, the industrial revolution has never been a vast satanic mystery taking place in some distant slum like Scranton, Pennsylvania, but was something that you can hold in the hand and plug into the wall socket in the living room – or the bedroom or the bathroom. Much of the revolutionary fascination of a designer like Eames or of film directors like Godard or Dick Lester, or the new generation of pop record producers comes from the sense that they are so at home with their technology that they can afford to muck about – hence all the fun and games with distortion and feedback on Beatles or Jimi Hendrix records, because perfect reproduction you can almost take for granted. Distortion now takes an act of will.

But parallel with this liberating development of portable hand sized technology has come the growth of an invisible technology. The transistor radio depends on a distribution system without any physical channels at all, the power for the hand drill comes out of a mysterious hole in the wall, but more than this, all our bulky services that can go underground or into the wall are going there so fast that you can almost see them going. At the beginning of this century, most rooms were heated by apparatus big enough to add up to major architectural features – fire places, stoves, massive hot water radiators. But now the heating has gone into the floor slab or the skirting. All that remains visible is the thermostat.

Changes of this kind demand a recognition of the fact that the classic approach to industrial design is no longer valid: whether that classic approach was, say, an Ulm student refining a product till it was indistinguishable from any other Ulm product, or Harley Earl restyling a Buick right round the bend, the approach was still simply the reworking of a given product. As Michael Browne said with justifiable alarm about one Ulm project, 'All this research on paint brushes – did nobody discover that the paint roller might be a better answer?'

The answer was that they didn't: the programme of work set to the students, for all its violently different ideological background, was little different in its fundamental orientation from that which General Motors set the Buick stylists. Both visualised a giant industrial mechanism, remote from the life and control of the ultimate consumer, with the designer or stylist acting as an intermediary or interpreter between the two.

There has been little chance to see how right or wrong Ulm might have been, but the way in which Detroit got crossed up is already legendary. It was a GM executive who ruefully conceded 'We've given up mass producing cars; all we make now is interchangeable options.' And Ford had to advertise its Mustang as 'the car you design yourself' partly to bamboozle the customers into buying speed equipment they would never need, but equally in recognition of the fact that the customer is no longer prepared to accept the product as the factory hands it out, he wants to intervene personally in the creative process.

That this intervention is still relatively slight and does not involve working with the hands does not make the intervention any less real and significant. Insistence on a kind of absolute dichotomy (black/white good/evil) between machine production and handicraft can blind us to what is actually happening.

At the beginning of the fifties, for instance, the authors of *The Lonely Crowd* registered alarm at the intrusions of big business into the hot rod movement (which they seem to have known about only through papers written by other sociologists). They appeared to prefer to see hot-rodders as a tribe of noble savages laboriously making all their special speed equipment by hand – an idyll that the manufacturers of adaptors, converters, and other specialised off-the-peg equipment could only corrupt and impoverish. Somewhere in such arguments there is also usually implied a belief that there should always be absolute originality of design as well as absolute craftsmanship. Both have been set up as the only alternatives to the passive consumer of standardised goods, but if you look into a field like hot-rodding, or the rather similar one of slot car racing, you will see that one way out of this dilemma lies in not being so bloody absolute about it.

In both cases the vehicles are largely assembled from selections permuted from a very wide range of ready made components, standardised (but highly specialised) accessories and ingenious bolt-on or drop-in adaptors. The adaptors are designed to mate these special devices to one another or to basic standard automotive parts, or to mate basic standard parts from different contexts (Ford engine, Chevrolet gear box, Chrysler drive train, etc) into workable combinations. The slot-racing maniac disposes of a similar, or even wider, range of standard chassis, motors, gear sets, body shells, wheels, and tyres.

The fundamental skill required to exploit this cornucopia creatively is not so much a quick hand with the spanner and screwdriver as a mental information-retrieval system that will send you at once to the right catalogue for the particular whatsit that will unite the components into the dream vehicle you have in mind. It might be an extremely obscure gear set from Japan, available only from a shop in Lewisham, that makes it possible to get a really hot Mabuchi tin can motor into an Airfix Mini-minor body shell; or it might be the dress-up wheel discs from the relevant page of the Warshawsky catalogue that will finalise the conversion of your savagely chopped-about Impala into an underground joke about Cadillacs.

But to achieve this there will in nearly every case remain a modicum of actual original and manual craftsmanship needed to make some special fit-up that isn't in the catalogue. In general however there is no nonsense about working everything up from basic raw materials – no one in this connection is going lengthily and laboriously to carve a crankshaft from a solid billet with a hacksaw while reading about half Gibbon's *Decline and Fall* like Geoffrey Taylor of Alta Cars did.

The important thing is that in neither case is the product an end in itself, it is a means of winning races, or picking up girls, or astounding your friends, or enraging the middle aged. It is, in any case, a means to an end too specialised to be satisfied by a straightforward mass produced object, and too exacting to be satisfied by amateur lashups. Whatever earnest post-Ruskinian theorists may have feared about the professionalisation of hot-rodding and the corruption of its practitioners, this curious mixture of the personal and the prefabricated, the standard and the special has probably given more genuine self-expression and more self-fulfilment to more hot-rodders than any amount of totally original craftsmanship would have done. We aren't all endowed with absolute originality, we have different talents differently arranged: a situation like this enables you to concentrate on your areas of talent and get the rest done by experts. You can make up as much of an original lifestyle as you want and conform where you feel the need.

It is in situations like this that we can begin to discern ways in which post-industrial society can break out of the cast iron prison of the factory system. Whether you see the smaller, handier, less obstructive, more adaptable machinery as a symbol, a symptom, or a signpost, it remains a portent that we had better attend to.

At this point I must acknowledge that there is a substantial body of opinion – and there has been, ever since David Riesman masterminded the writing of *The Lonely Crowd* – which doubts if these technological freedoms and self fulfillments are worth having if they leave the system – meaning the political structure – undisturbed. There is, for instance, a very large worry going round that computerisation and information handling techniques are going to intensify the detail and closeness with which our lives are scrutinised and supervised by the powers that be. The fear ranges over large areas of human life, from the students who wear pins saying 'I am a human being, do not fold, staple or mutilate me' to the businessman who realises that the computerisation of Old Mother Barclay makes his current balance so rapidly known to so many bank officials that several credit-storming techniques are no longer of service to him.

But the real reason, I suspect, why the spread of electronic control networks causes such alarm is that its operations are invisible. Like domestic heating systems, social control systems are disappearing into the floor slab. Whereas the reduced obstrusiveness of modern heating can help to disencumber our living space, the reduced obstrusiveness of social controls simply reduces the number of sensitive targets on which opposition or reform can exert pressure. Above all, the traditional handicraft methods of expressing opinion – stoning Christian saints, assassinating tyrants, storming bastilles, building barricades – are ineffective because the structure of power has ceased to be open to that kind of manual manipulation. Let's face it, the reason

last October's great demo went off so quietly was that Tariq Ali and the breakaway group who went to Grosvenor Square decided to express their opposition by means of techniques that wouldn't have seemed very modern to the Chartists. They thus left the power structure where – I suspect – they wanted it, intact for further assaults at a later time.

The techniques required to divert or disrupt the new invisible power system are all, probably, simple. But they require the use of the head, not the hand, and they significantly do not offer the comforts of rousing, soul stirring mass action. All these techniques depend on an appreciation of the nature of the networks on which the new power depends. They are, by definition (and by observation) very extensive, elaborately cross linked, and easily accessible. The number of sick jokes about atomic disasters precipitated by breaks in the present single hot line between Washington and Moscow reveals a widespread appreciation of the fact that simple linear communications are inadequate to the emergencies of our complex technological world. There must be instant methods of bypassing breaks. Hence the cross-linkages – and hence my suspicion that an offshore airport connected to England only by a monorail will finish up as either a desert or a deathtrap.

But these extended and complex networks must be open to access by all and sundry if they are to signal emergencies rapidly enough, or to distribute information to as many unexpected places as necessary. No police force, for instance, can operate on its own private communications networks alone but needs a network open to public channels as well: communist states must tolerate the security risks inherent in having a network of radio amateurs all over eastern Europe (remember Czechoslovakia!) because they never know when some national or military disaster might make them indispensable.

It is the accessibility and complexity of these networks which lets individual activity back into the deal. You can beat the system because (a) the system can't keep you out and (b) it is so necessarily complex that you can't immediately be found out when you have got in. When you consider how long it takes the telephone system to clear itself of a simple psychopathic obscenity-fancier or the various heavy breathers who used to call up girls in Chelsea you begin to see what the possibilities are for striking the odd blow for freedom if you are part of an intelligent and determined group of saboteurs or Yippies.

The essential is to be able to identify adjacent sensitive points in the relevant networks – especially points where networks interlink – and bear down on them simultaneously. Give me a day when the Prime Minister is away from the red telephones of state and I can cut him off from the decision making process with only half a dozen helpers. Remember the CND project for mass toilet flushing? Actually there's too much spare capacity in both the water-supply and sewage disposal systems, but a mass switch on of every electrical appliance within reach would duplicate the great New York blackout in any heavily urbanised area. Or, in a more bloodthirsty vein, because a lot of people would be wounded, crushed, or suffocated, give me the Thursday evening rush hour and a hundred student activists and I can wreck London.

You don't have to be a mechanical whizz kid to produce this kind of positive triumph of people over mechanisms, of software over the hardware network. All you need is nerve and natural cunning. Example: the access to central parking lots in a certain US university was restricted to a few privileged deans and professors who gained admittance by pushing into a gate control slot an identity card with a code of invisible magnetic dots along its edge. Members of the physics department soon broke the code and got to work forging cards. The code was changed, broken again, and so on. Soon a considerable part of the human and physical resources of the physics department was devoted to code smashing. The art department then took over and solved the problem once and for all, without electronic sensors, computers or anything. They produced a card with a continuous magnetic strip right along the edge, a magnetic skeleton key against which there was no defence because it corresponded to all conceivable patterns of dots.

But the distributive networks of our life cover more than communication systems. We have already gone a long way in the process of spreading our powered equipment evenly over the face of the land. By the nineteen fifties the average – *average* – household in Europe disposed of the same horsepower rating of mechanisms as a European industrial worker in 1900. Much of this horsepower is under used – it would work far more productively and continuously than at present (it is daft to have a washing machine standing still six days a week) and it could do a greater variety of things. The same ingenuity that works out a universal forged parking ticket can also put the existing provision of domestic power services to convert the bathroom into a photographic darkroom, and then convert that darkroom into a pharmaceutical laboratory capable of producing first class bootleg LSD. In fact it is doubtful whether bathtub LSD can ever be controlled, let alone eradicated. The consequence of making people clean enough to be socially tolerable is to equip them to produce sophisticated drugs. And after bathtub LSD how far away is the backyard atom bomb?

All this could represent a major redistribution of effective social power. Existing networks of command and information gathering are becoming inadequate, even to the companies who produce the equipment that is producing these revolutions. So distinguished electronic companies, raised in the aura of grey flannel suits and grey crackle finish cabinet work, now have to put up with long haired flower people raving it up in their boardrooms in a cloud of incense or cannabis fumes, because this is the only way they can find out what the hell ever happens to their product when it gets out into the market – partly because the market is inaccessible to ordinary market research techniques, partly because the market is using the equipment to do things that never occurred to its original designers.

Every electronic company now needs a company freak either on the payroll or as a reclining consultant. This situation is going to become more general as the software becomes more and more at home with the hardware, as we begin to realise that mechanisms can be mastered, and they do not have to master us. I wouldn't like to say what's cause and what's effect; whether handier hardware teaches people to be more demanding, or whether more demanding software summons up handier machinery, but the effects are becoming clear. What happens when electronic amplification meets an uninhibited Liverpool poet? The result is Adrian Henri spouting a kind of verse that could not work under any other circumstances: verse verbal and oral, using the rhythms of speech and the reinforcing effects of repetitions that would be intolerable and boring in print, but a verse that at the same time is often so delicate that it would die the death if it were shouted loud enough to be heard at the back of the room without electronic boosting. Conversely he could produce bludgeoning decibel levels in his anti-war Batman poems that were beyond the range of human shout. Great. This is the kind of triumph of software which we can all afford to applaud; these are the strains of creativity proper to a world of electronic hardware.

This present mood of the hardware users seems to demand of designers unconventional intuitions in order to provide a break out from the presently accepted rationalistic methods of conceiving designs. We still proceed by the classic method, which I suppose goes back to Descartes, in some way, of isolating a function, devising a mechanism to serve that function, and then progressively refining that mechanism. Within this process the industrial designer has usually manifested himself at a late stage among the refinements. The result of this method, which – like the division of labour – happens to suit the primitive, monumental, concentrated phase of the factory system, is to cause a proliferation of refined and highly specialised single function objects which are never quite able to replace their predecessors. The primitive hearth becomes a cooker with a battery of highly differentiated heating elements – grill, boiler, simmerstat, oven toaster and a primitive hearth for barbecuing. The primitive sink becomes a dishwasher, an automated clothes washer *and* a sink still. The larder becomes a fridge, a deep freeze *and* a larder.

Yet this is the inevitable outcome of the sentiment which we have all applauded in Le Corbusier when he said of the problem of designing an aeroplane: 'To wish to fly like a bird was to state the problem badly... to search for a means of support and a means of propulsion was to put the problem properly.' Reductive reasoning of this kind has provided most of the major advances of western technology so far, but are we – in face of a less acquiescent body of consumers – reaching the point where reductive reasoning is getting in its own way; when the monofunction fully automated toaster has been so perfected that it will produce a slice of bread evenly and delicately browned on both sides – but only when fed with purpose designed bread of standard texture and moisture machined to slice-thickness tolerances of plus or minus five thou.

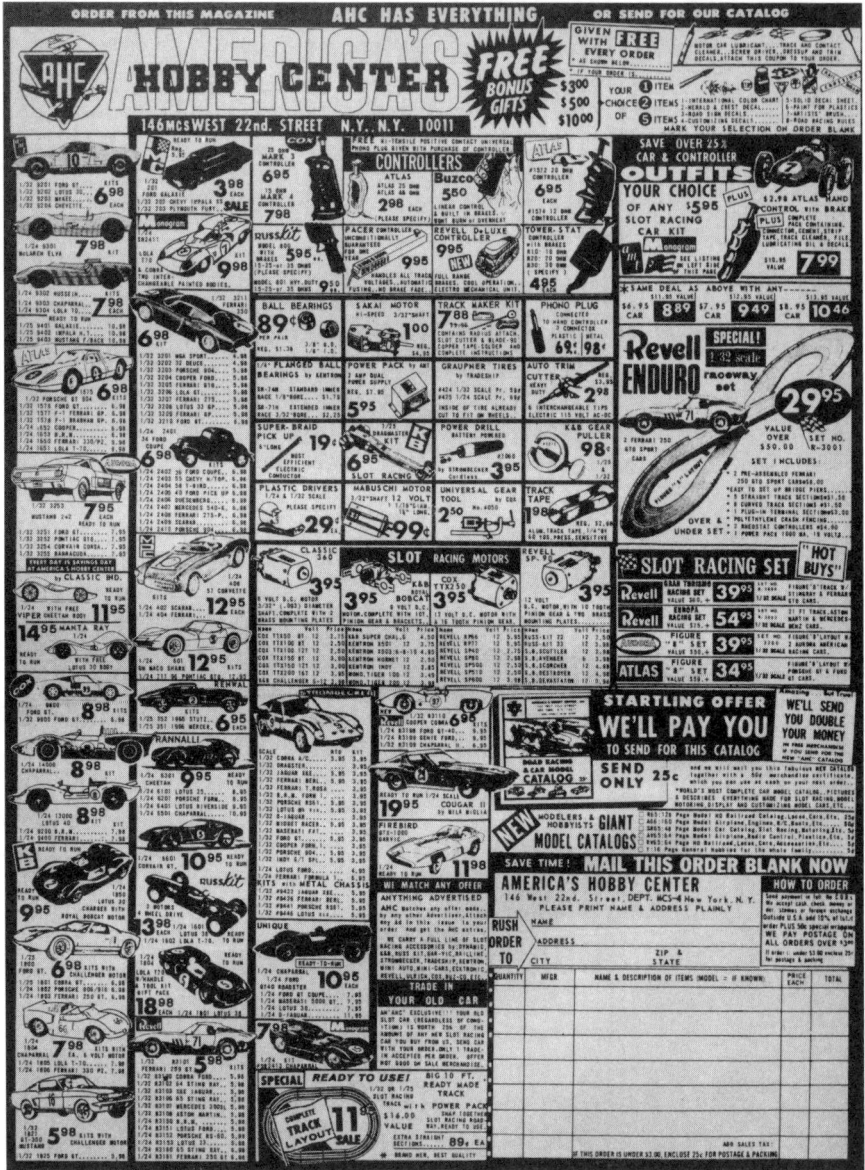

Page reproduction from *Model Car* magazine.

The fact that this is a rational approach does not mean that it is the *only* rational approach. It would be equally rational to identify common aspects of all functions and to make a nearly universal machine to perform them all by the aid of specialised accessories – which is already beginning to happen with gear like kitchen mixers. Or it might be equally rational to go back to square one – the original undifferentiated sink, say – and ask what makes it so adaptable. The answer, I suspect, is the ingenious adaptability of the human user – how about mechanising that – or at least making the human user a paradigm of the level of adaptability required of an operating machine.

Either of these would be a triumph of software in the sense of the liberation of human beings from boring or repetitive tasks, their liberation from the fixed image and fixed functional aspect of equipment as currently designed. Liberation of this kind appears to be psychologically and culturally important right now. For instance, the Italian architectural magazines last year were buzzing with the aftermath of a speech by Giulio Carlo Argan in which he said 'we are alienated from our objects'. Several commentators guessed this to mean that designed objects no longer have the impact they did a decade ago when an Eames chair, a Braun mixer, a Citroen OS 19 looked like manifestations of a future golden age. I think the gloss can go further; we are alienated even from these classic objects by their perfect boring reliability.

The significant and memorable products of the present time nearly all contain elements of surprise, of variability, of exploitable imperfection. But then those products are not finite designed objects. Expressed in a jumbo cliche, they are interdeterminate participatory open ended situations – be they a TV discussion that gets out of hand, a free university, an adventure playground, an autodestructive sculpture – or certain hardy perennials like love affairs and raising families.

Our object-world offers little that is remotely comparable: what it offers mostly is a succession of discrete, fixed, timeless objects to a world which has begun to rediscover the reunifying virtues of the footloose flow of time in motion. The kind of object which registers as anything more than an over-styled servant in this context must be able to symbolise what is really at stake. Hence the fascination of temporarily rallying structures – Archigram's walking city or an inflatable dome – which mark the point in time where we meet to participate in this or that, and then move on. Or, to turn from the collective to the individual, the fascination of the customised car, which binds time and technology – new machinery in old body shell, new paint job and antique accessories – in a personal statement which is, in some vital though often hidden essential, as unique as its maker; symbol of our growing but barely understood capacity to shift the whole balance between men and their objects, to mould the world of equipment nearer to heart's desire.

Many of the points made in this article were first presented in an address to the Design and Industries Association Annual Conference, 1969.

Page reproduction from the Warshawsky catalogue.

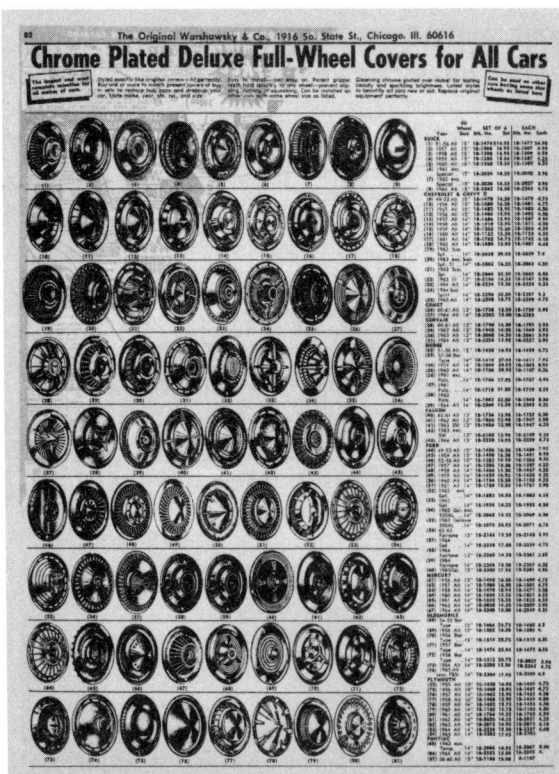

Photographs by Reyner Banham

Within the archives at the Architectural Association there are around 2,000 colour photographs taken by Reyner Banham, recording visits to projects in London, Norwich and Milton Keynes as well as his travels around the United States. Arcosanti, Philip Johnson's AT&T building and the Barbican feature alongside dams and grain elevators; construction details alongside desert canyons. The collection provides something of a glimpse through Banham's eye, into his interests and his attentions.

pp 66–7   (Left) Alexandra Road Development in London, designed by Neave Brown, completed in 1968 and photographed in 1978.

(Right) Detail of Lake Shore Drive Apartments in Chicago, Illinois, designed by Mies van der Rohe, completed in 1951 and photographed in 1986.

pp 68–9   (Left) Fountain Paint Pot in Yellowstone National Park, Wyoming, photographed in 1978.

(Right) TVA Fontana Storage Dam across the Little Tennessee River in North Carolina, completed in 1945 and photographed in 1977.

pp 70–1   (Left) Kresge College at the University of California, Santa Cruz, designed by Moore, Lyndon, Turnbull and Whitaker, completed in 1973 and photographed in 1983.

(Right) Exterior canopy detail of Fawcett House in Los Banos, California, designed by Frank Lloyd Wright, completed in 1955 and photographed in 1980.

Mimi Zeiger
Cheeseburger in Paradise

//

Reyner Banham
Architecture II: Fantastic

Published in *Los Angeles: The Architecture of Four Ecologies*, 1971, pp 110–35.

Mimi Zeiger
Cheeseburger in Paradise

Published a year after *Los Angeles: The Architecture of Four Ecologies* (1971), *Learning from Las Vegas* gets more credit for ushering in postmodernism than the earlier text. Duck versus Decorated Shed holds fast in architectural consciousness as a diagram of symbolic form. (That duck, of course, lifted and détourned from the pages of *God's Own Junkyard*, Peter Blake's 1964 elegy on the American landscape.) Banham's chapter 'Architecture II: Fantastic', however, delivers an equally precise analysis of pop architecture.

In looking at the everyday buildings that make up the sprawling urbanism of greater LA, Banham draws distinctions between symbolic and functional form with the most delicious of metaphors: the hamburger. Like a piece of American cheese glued to a bun, he melds together the everyday, greasy fast-food item with the city's cinematic legacy under the rubric of fantasy, then spends the opening paragraphs of the chapter laying out an ode to the sit-down hamburger served not-wrapped in paper but on a platter. 'Its component parts have been carefully opened up and separated out into an assemblage of functional and symbolic elements, or alternatively, a fantasia on functional themes.'

On the burger theme, Eve Babitz, writer, it-girl and Angeleno, cites *Los Angeles* in her 1974 memoir *Eve's Hollywood*: 'It makes the city make sense and I bought it for a rock-and-roll friend, who was complaining one day about LA and how he wanted to move into the country, so now he's transformed, he's trying to get an apartment in the flats and out of the hills and the more McDonald's Hamburgery it is, the better he likes it. It is, then, something when someone can make you see beauty where you only saw ugliness before.'

The writing is particularly luscious, dripping with Tom Wolfe influence and New Journalism stylings. Indeed, he even evokes Wolfe's neologism, 'electrographic architecture', when praising the grandiose neon signage deployed by commercial buildings. Banham introduces terminology to parse the varying pretenses of Los Angeles' obsession with fantasy: Custom, Decorator and Gourmet. These terms, lost or never adopted within architectural parlance, are still with us as marketing signifiers of status and lifestyle.

And the metaphor of the hamburger punctuates the chapter from the *Gestalt* interiority of the Brown Derby restaurant to the spires of Watts Towers. Yet, if there is a blind spot in Banham's tour, it is in the unreserved celebration of Simon Rodia's hand-built towers, which are presented as a fantastic example of public architecture without ever addressing the structure's context and cultural condition. Rodia, an Italian immigrant, scrapped together his construction from rebar, broken crockery and 7-Up bottles, building from this bricolage a structure that would come to represent a monument of Black culture and anticipate an Afrofuturist imaginary. (Legend holds that when king-of-Pop Andy Warhol visited LA the only place he wanted to see was Watts Towers.) In 1965, just six years before *Los Angeles* was published, the Watts Rebellion shook the Black neighbourhood, leaving scars of racial segregation and police violence that are still with us today. That's a hard reality that no embrace of fantasy – no cheeseburger in paradise, no Disneyland, no Tahitian Village Motel – can possibly erase.

REYNER BANHAM
ARCHITECTURE II: FANTASTIC

Like the film, the hamburger is a non-Californian invention that has achieved a kind of symbolic apotheosis in Los Angeles; symbolic, that is, of the way fantasy can lord it over function in Southern California. The purely functional hamburger, as delivered across the counter of say, the Gipsy Wagon on the UCLA campus, the Surf-boarder at Hermosa Beach or any McDonald's or Jack-in-the-Box outlet anywhere, is a pretty well-balanced meal that he who runs (surfs, drives, studies) can eat with one hand; not only the ground beef but all the sauce, cheese, shredded lettuce, and other garnishes are firmly gripped between the two halves of the bun.

But the fantastic hamburger as served on a platter at a sit-down restaurant is something else again. Its component parts have been carefully opened up and separated out into an assemblage of functional and symbolic elements, or alternatively, a fantasia on functional themes. The two halves of the bun lie face up with the ground beef on one and, sometimes, the cheese on the other. Around and alongside on the platter are the lettuce leaves, gherkins, onion rings, fried potatoes, paper cups of relish or coleslaw, pineapple rings, and much more besides, because the invention of new varieties of hamburger is a major Angeleno culinary art. Assembled with proper care it can be a work of visual art as well; indeed, it must be considered as visual art first and foremost, since some components are present in too small a quantity generally to make a significant gustatory as opposed to visual contribution – for instance the seemingly mandatory ring of red-dyed apple, which does a lot for the eye as a foil to the general greenery of the salads, but precious little for the palate.

The way in which the functional and symbolic parts of the hamburger platter have been discriminated, separated, and displayed is a fair analogue for the design of most of the buildings in which they are sold. No nonsense about integrated design, every part conceived in separated isolation and made the most of; the architecture of symbolic assemblage. But it was not always so; the earlier architecture of commercial fantasy of the city tended to yield primacy to a single symbolic form or *Gestalt* into which everything had to be fitted. The famous Brown Derby restaurant in the shape of a hat, the Cream Cans (in the shape of cream cans), the Hoot Hoot I Scream outlet (in the form of an owl, not an ice-cream) and the several Bonzo dogs that sold hot dogs in the twenties and thirties, repackaged their functional propositions in symbolic envelopes expressing a single, formal idea.

The building and the symbol are one and the same thing, and if this sounds like one of the approved aims of architecture as a fine art, then it can certainly be paralleled in the work of reputable art architects of the period and later – Henry Oliver's Spadina house of 1925, with its domestic functions re-packaged in a Hansel and Gretel image, or almost any Angeleno building where a single idea has been made dominant over everything else, most triumphantly, perhaps, in Lloyd Wright's Wayfarer's Chapel of 1949, which contrives to command respect both as architecture in the respectable sense of the word, and as Pop fantasy comparable to the wilder kind of gourmet-style restaurants.

Such symbolic packaging within a single conceptual form can impose strains even on a building with one function only to serve, let alone a multiplicity of functions, and there were always needs that drove fantasists in other directions. So Grauman's Chinese Theatre, the ultimate shrine of all the fantasy that was Hollywood, kept most of its fantastication as a garnish for the façade and the pavilions flanking Meyer and Holler's generous forecourt, while the architecture underneath is plain bread-and-butter stuff like the buns of the hamburger. It is, indeed, a much less 'integrated design' than either of its two most celebrated fantastic contemporaries, both by Morgan Wall and Clements, the Assyrian-style Samson Rubber Company plant, and the recently demolished black-and-gold Richfield Building downtown. But one other properly appliquéed fantasy does survive from the twenties: the totally improbable Aztec Hotel in Monrovia; intended by its designer to be Mayan rather than Aztec, it has his supposedly Mayan detailing stuck all over a relatively plain structure like piped icing on a pastry.

Fantasy is actually found only rarely in the planning of a building, or the layout of adjoining clustered structures – even a much later fantasy such as the Bel Air hotel, laid out like a Spanish Colonial Revival village, finally proves to be a rational system of pedestrian courts – the real fantasy there is the 'outdoor' fireplace under a tree in a rockery at the end of the dining-room. Fantasy of the hamburger kind is all too often a compensation for the poverty of the building behind or under it, or for the hard-nosed rationalism of the market economy, and this division between the rational, functional shell and the fantastic garnish has become more apparent as the years have passed. On Wilshire Boulevard, and over a time-span of a decade, the development can be seen in the two prime department stores. Bullock's-Wilshire has an eye-catching tower that grows naturally out of the detailing and structural rhythms of what is below, an immensely professional piece of architecture by Parkinson and Parkinson in 1929; May Company at the end of Miracle Mile has its equally eye-catching gilt cylinder chopped back into the corner of a rectangular shopping-box to which it is related only by physical attachment, Albert C Martin in 1939 having turned in a piece of immensely professional store-planning, but not architecture in the earlier sense.

The next stage of the development can be seen, still on Wilshire, just across Fairfax Avenue from May Company; Johnies, which actually does sell hamburgers. Somewhere underneath the fantasy lurks a plain rectangular flat-roofed building, around which a purely notional butterfly roof has been sketched, but turned down front and back to give a sheltering form not unlike the nominal mansard roofs that give the name to the Gourmet Mansardic style of restaurant architecture. On the front this roof is garnished with lettering, and the whole structure is flanked by entirely independent signs, one merely lettered, the other humorously [sic] pictorial. And a crowning non sequitur – an enormous sign which is part of the structure but advertises something entirely different.

The lower down the scales of financial substance and cultural pretensions one goes, the better sense it apparently makes (and has made, visibly, for a couple of decades) to buy a plain standard building shell from Butler Buildings Corporation or a similar mass-producer and add symbolic garnish to the front, top, or other parts that show. It makes even better sense, of course, to acquire an existing disused building and impose your commercial personality on it with symbolic garnishes. But even if you are a major commercial operator with a chain of outlets, even a major oil company, it still makes financial sense to put up relatively simple single-storey boxes, and then make them tall enough to attract attention by piling up symbols and graphic art on top. So Jack-in-the-Box heaps storey heights of graphics and symbols on top of quite simple and unassumingly functional drive-by hamburger bars; or a big supermarket may even run up an entirely independent sign detached from any building, and make it a visually interesting structure in its own right, like the double-tapered lattice tower at Norwalk Square.

But having proposed this sliding scale of commercial frugality versus cultural or aesthetic status, I have to admit some major anomalies that spoil the graph – though this is fair enough in the realm of fantasy. Many banks, despite their manifest status as monuments to the most enduring cultural values of a frankly acquisitive way of life, make a strong pitch at the Pop commercial level. Sometimes – as with the notorious applied art work of the Ahmanson Banks – it is possible to suspect such a confusion of cultural intentions as to make further discussion pointless (though no less humorous), but there are a few bank buildings which are designed exactly by the rules discussed above. The best example is the Cabrillo Savings Bank building on the Pacific Coast Highway at Torrance, which has a three-storey-high arcaded porch *à la* Yamasaki (for which the local source would be Ed Stone's Perpetual Savings Banks) and clearly functioning as a symbol of superior cultural tone, but entirely separate from the single-storey bank building around which it is wrapped, a total discrimination between the functional and symbolic parts of the design.

The other and more interesting area of anomalies embraces the architecture of restaurants, where these have any pretensions above the level of burger bars or coffee shops. There is a fairly well-defined middle level of domestic affluence in Los Angeles whose presence can be identified by certain key adjectives used in advertising to signify the kind of pretension that is also common in the middle rank of restaurants. These are *Custom* ('custom view homes'), *Decorator* ('antiqued decorator bar-stools'), and *Gourmet* ('gourmet party dips'). Within its own field the last has such precise status, outranking *Delicatessen* by the same degree that *Delicatessen* outranks *grocery*, that it seems entirely appropriate to adopt *Gourmet* as the stylistic label for the more aspiring kind of restaurant architecture.

Crenshaw Ford Agency, 1967.

Johnies Wilshire, Miracle Mile, 1962.

Brown Derby restaurant, Wilshire Boulevard, 1926.

Architecture II: Fantastic

From the Brown Derby onwards, through the Velvet Turtle at Redondo Beach, and onwards into a plushly under-lit future of 'Total Meal Experience', restaurants have been the most intensely and completely designed buildings in the area – few, even, of the most expensive houses can have had so much detailed attention devoted to them inside and out, and some of Rudolph Schindler's most inventive and advanced design was inside the Sardi's he did in 1932. In their current incarnations, they tend to be dark, both in terms of levels of illumination and the colour of woodwork, floor-coverings (often tiles or brick) and other integral surfaces, much subdivided by pierced screens or theatrically focused on a massive open fire-hearth or two.

Grauman's Chinese Theatre, Hollywood, 1927, Meyer and Holler, architects.

This kind of Gourmet/Decorator interior is common in other parts of the US, of course; the Los Angeles variant differs in its greater reliance on Spanish Colonial sources (including one or two genuine pre-1848 pieces of furniture if possible) but chiefly in being done with greater skill, resourcefulness, and conviction. The same is true of the gourmet exterior in its two chief local varieties. The 'Gracious Living' variant often recalls the kind of nineteenth-century architecture that Professor Hitchcock categorised as 'Second Empire and Cognate Modes' slightly compromised by Hudson River Bracketted. To the front of the standard lightweight rectangular building shell this style adds round-arched openings, thin pretty detailing such as balconies and the small, steeply pitched false roof-fronts that justify the stylistic epithet Gourmet Mansardic.

The 'Char-broiled Protein' variant, on the other hand, has its ultimate sources in the ranch-house style, locally modified by the influence of the Greene Brothers and Frank Lloyd Wright, and shaggy surfaces that have the same implications of masculinity as an unshaven chin; massive rough-tiled roofs pulled well down and well out beyond the building envelope, exposed and roughly finished timber within and without, supplemented by random rubble or field-stone for exposed structural columns and the open hearths which are, of course, fundamental to the whole style – even to the extent of being supplemented by purely symbolic fire-pits under metal hoods on the outside of the building in some examples. Planning variations within the style extend from the endlessly informal to neatly balanced pairs of pavilions under 'mausoleum' roofs, Philadelphia-style, and the whole manner reaches one of its most notable local extremes in the so-called Polynesian restaurants.

In terms of geographical distribution, as well as stylistic pretensions, the Polynesians are everywhere from High-Gourmet 'Restaurant Row' next to Gallery Row on La Cienega Boulevard, to your local neighbourhood shopping centre. Epitomised by, say, the Tahitian Village in Bellflower, it exhibits a high, peaky roof pulled out across the side-walk in a long pointed gable that must owe more, ultimately, to Saarinen's Hockey Rink than to anything in the South Seas, and a profusion of carved wood and rough hewn surfaces (even the risers of the external steps have been distressed with a trowel before the cement was dry) buried in a positive green salad of impenetrable exotic evergreens.

A building as strikingly and lovably ridiculous as this represents well enough the way Los Angeles sums up a general phenomenon of US life; the convulsions in building style that follow when traditional cultural and social restraints have been overthrown and replaced by the preferences of a mobile, affluent, consumer-oriented society, in which 'cultural values' and ancient symbols are handled primarily as methods of claiming or establishing status. This process has probably gone further in, say, Las Vegas, yet it is in the context of Los Angeles that everyone seems to feel the strongest compulsion to discuss this fantasticating tendency.

And rightly so. Until Las Vegas became unashamedly middle-aged and the boring Beaux-Arts Caesars' Palace was built, its architecture was an extreme suburban variant of Los

Jack-in-the-Box hamburger stand.

Angeles – Douglas Honnold, now a respected doyen of the architectural profession in Los Angeles, worked for Bugsy Siegel in the design of the Flamingo, the pioneer casino-hotel on the Strip. Las Vegas has been as much a marginal gloss on Los Angeles as was Brighton Pavilion on Regency London. More important, Los Angeles has seen in this century the greatest concentration of fantasy-production, as an industry and as an institution, in the history of Western man. In the guise of Hollywood as well as other causes, Los Angeles gave us the movies as we know them and stamped its image on the infant television industry. And stemming from the impetus given by Hollywood as well as other causes, Los Angeles is also the home of the most extravagant myths of private gratification and self-realisation, institutionalised now in the doctrine of 'doing your own thing'.

Both Hollywood's marketable commercial fantasies, and those private ones which are above or below calculable monetary value, have left their marks on the Angel City, but Hollywood brought something that all other fantasists needed – technical skill and resources in converting fantastic ideas into physical realities. Since living flesh-and-blood actors and dancers had to walk through or prance upon Hollywood's fantasies, there was much that could not be accomplished with painted back-cloths or back-projections; much of Shangri-la had to be built in three dimensions, the spiral ramps of the production numbers of Busby Berkeley musical spectaculars had to support the weight of a hundred girls in silver top hats, and so on...

The movies were thus a peerless school for building fantasy as fact, and the facts often survived one movie to live again in another, and another and others still to come. Economy in using increasingly valuable acreage on studio-lots caused these fantastic façades and ancient architectures reproduced in plaster to be huddled together into what have become equally fantastic townscapes which not only survive as cities of romantic illusion, but have been elevated to the status of a kind of cultural monument, which now form the basis for tourist excursions more flourishing than the traditional tours of film-stars' homes.

This business of showing the plant to visitors as a tourist attraction has spread beyond the movie industry, into such monuments of public relations as the Busch Gardens in the

San Fernando Valley, where the real-life brewery is only one of the features shown, and back into the movie industry with Disneyland – the set for a film that was never ever going to be made except in the mind of the visitor. In creating this compact sequence of habitable fantasies, WED Enterprises seem to have transcended Hollywood, Los Angeles, Walt Disney's original talents and all other identifiable ingredients of this environmental phantasmagoria.

In terms of an experience one can walk or ride through, inhabit and enjoy, it is done with such consummate skill and such base cunning that one can only compare it to something completely outrageous, like the brothel in Genet's *Le Balcon*. It is an almost faultless organisation for delivering, against cash, almost any type at all of environmental experience that human fancy, however inflamed, could ever devise. Here are pedestrian piazzas, seas, jungles, castles, outer space, Main Street, the old West, mountains, more than can be experienced in a single day's visit... and all embraced within some obvious ironies, as all institutionalised fantasies must be.

The greatest of these ironies has to do with transportation, and this underlies the brothel comparison. Set in the middle of a city obsessed with mobility, a city whose most characteristic festival is the Rose Parade in Pasadena, fantastically sculptured Pop inventions entirely surfaced with live flowers rolling slowly down Colorado Boulevard every New Year's Day – in this city Disneyland offers illicit pleasures of mobility. Ensconced in a sea of giant parking-lots in a city devoted to the automobile, it provides transportation that does not exist outside – steam trains, monorails, people-movers, tram-trains, travelators, ropeways, not to mention pure transport fantasies such as simulated space-trips and submarine rides. Under-age children, too young for driver's licences, enjoy the licence of driving on their own freeway system and adults can step off the pavement and mingle with the buses and trams on Main Street in a manner that would lead to sudden death or prosecution outside.

But more than this, the sheer concentration of different forms of mechanical movement means that Disneyland is almost the only place where East Coast town-planning snobs, determined that their cities shall never suffer the automotive 'fate' of Los Angeles, can bring their students or their city

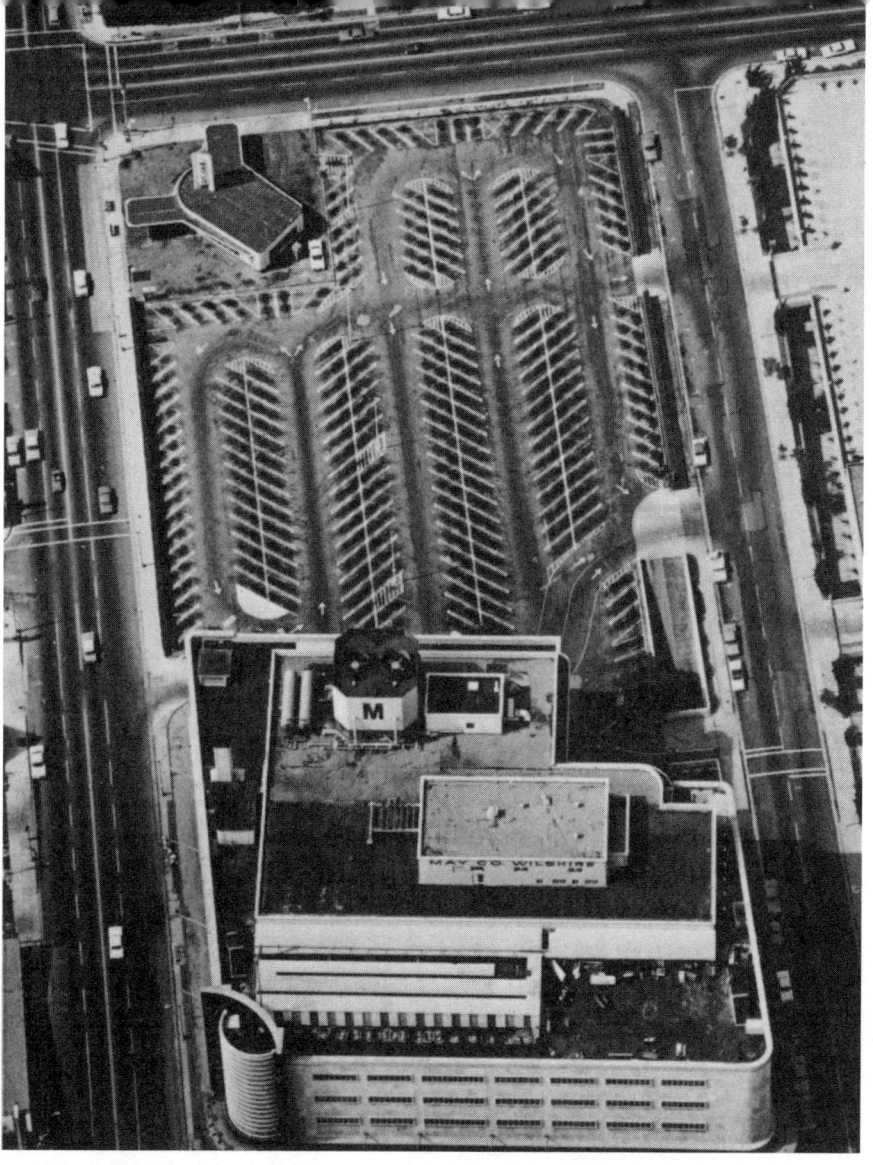

May Company, Miracle Mile, 1939, Albert C Martin and Associates, architects. Photograph Ed Ruscha, *May Company, 6067 Wilshire Blvd*, from the series *Parking Lots*, 1967/1999 © Ed Ruscha.

councillors to see how the alternative might work in the flesh and metal – to this blatantly commercial fun-fair in the city they hate. And seeing how well it all worked, I began to understand the wisdom of Ray Bradbury in proposing that Walt Disney was the only man who could make rapid transit a success in Los Angeles. All the skill, cunning, salesmanship, and technical proficiency are there.

They are also at diametrical variance with the special brand of 'innocence' that underlies the purely personal fantasies of Los Angeles. Innocence is a word to use cautiously in this context, because it must be understood as not comprising either simplicity or ingenuousness. Deeply imbued with standard myths of the Natural Man and the Noble Savage, as in other parts of the US, this innocence grows and flourishes as an assumed right in the Southern California sun, an ingenious and technically proficient cult of private and harmless gratifications that is symbolised by the surfer's secret smile of intense concentration and the immensely sophisticated and highly decorated plastic surf-board he needs to conduct his private communion with the sea.

This fantasy of innocence has one totally self-absorbed and perfected monument in Los Angeles, so apt, so true and so imaginative that it has gained the world-wide fame it undoubtedly deserves: Simon Rodia's clustered towers in Watts. Alone of the buildings of Los Angeles they are almost too well known to need description, tapering traceries of coloured pottery shards bedded in cement on frames of scrap steel and baling wire. They are unlike anything else in the world – especially unlike all the various prototypes that have been proposed for them by historians who have never seen them in physical fact. Their actual presence is testimony to a genuinely original creative spirit.

And in the thirty-three years of absorbed labour he devoted to their construction, and in his uninhibited ingenuity in exploiting the by-products of an affluent technology, and in his determination to 'do something big', and in his ability to walk away when they were finished in 1954, Rodia was very much at one with the surfers, hot-rodders, sky-divers, and scuba-divers who personify the tradition of private, mechanistic *satori*-seeking in California. But he was also at variance with the general body of fantastic architecture thereabouts.

Watts Towers, 1921–54, Simon Rodia, inventor.

Architecture as a way of direct personal gratification like Rodia's rarely rises above the level of plaster-gnomery or home-is-where-the-heart-shaped-flower-bed-is. The towers of Watts are as unique as they are proper in Los Angeles, for the going body of architectural fantasy is in the public, not private, domain, and constitutes almost the only public architecture in the city – public in the sense that it deals in symbolic meanings the populace at large can read. Both fantasy and public symbolism reached their apotheosis in the great commercial signs, in the style of design that Tom Wolfe acclaimed, in his own neologism, as 'electrographic architecture' – that is, a combination of artificial light and graphic art that can even comprise a whole building. Wolfe's chosen examples in Los Angeles are the Crenshaw Ford Agency and the Crenshaw Mobil Station in which he sees, rightly, a move 'from mere lettering to whole structures designed primarily as pictures or representational sculpture'. Wild as these objects may appear, grotesque, ludicrous, stimulating or uplifting, they fit into an established local pattern of architectural invention that reaches deep into the city's history and style of life.

Historically, the tradition begins with the spires, not of Watts but of Westwood Village: illuminated needles capping cinemas and even banks in order to be seen from Wilshire Boulevard, which is only a quarter of a mile away, but which was not (in the twenties, when Westwood was subdivided) zoned for commercial uses. And this tradition also crowns the city's life-style, not only in commercial signs, but also in one structure that is a public building in the conventional sense of the word, the only public building in the whole city that genuinely graces the scene and lifts the spirit (and sits in firm control of the whole basis of human existence in Los Angeles): the Water and Power Building of 1964 by Albert C Martin and Associates. In daylight it is a conventional rectangular office block closing the end of an uninspired civic vista and standing in an altogether ordinary pool full of the usual fountains, but at night it is transformed. Darkness hides the boredoms of the civic centre and from the flanking curves of the freeways one sees only this brilliant cube of diamond-cool light riding above the lesser lights of downtown. It is the only gesture of public architecture that matches the style and scale of the city.

Water and Power Building, Los Angeles Civic Centre, 1963, Albert C Martin and Associates, architects.

Richard J Williams
The 'Spectacular Paradox' of Autopia

//

Reyner Banham
Ecology IV: Autopia

Published in *Los Angeles: The Architecture of Four Ecologies*, 1971, pp 213–22.

Richard J Williams
The 'Spectacular Paradox' of Autopia

'Autopia' is the eleventh chapter of Banham's 1971 book *Los Angeles: The Architecture of Four Ecologies*, and the fourth of the 'ecologies' of the book's title. The other three describe the city's defining landscapes: the beach, the Hollywood Hills and the flat plain between them. 'Autopia' describes the constructed landscape connecting them all – the freeway – and it is the most radical part of the book. Having dispensed with the freeway as architecture in an earlier chapter, 'The Transportation Palimpsest', Banham's concern here is the experience of freeway driving, and the claims he makes for it are certainly striking. The daily commute provides Angelenos with 'the two calmest and most rewarding hours of their daily lives', he writes; the freeway is nothing short of 'a special way of being alive'. The usual complaints about smog, congestion or accidents are exaggerated; far worse the experience of (then) British Rail's Southern Region. The freeways, he thinks, work 'uncommonly well'.

 Looking back at 'Autopia' at a half century's remove is to be reminded of why the freeways in LA and elsewhere were built in the first place. That they responded to booming automobile sales and traffic growth was quantifiable and obvious, along with well-documented pressure from the auto industry aligned with friendly politicians. But not often stated with such clarity was the way they formed and represented a set of pleasures. For Banham as much as the Beach Boys, freeway driving was its own reward. To maintain speed, to change lanes, to successfully navigate the sprawling network, were skills of a high order, and to use them successfully could be profoundly satisfying. It is good to be reminded of those pleasures now they are receding from the public imagination. The ongoing electrification of the automobile fleet, and its accompanying high level of automation of new cars suppose a driving experience in which old-fashioned driving pleasures have been eliminated. The car increasingly is supposed to drive itself; everyone is a passenger. And driving is now arguably too guilt-ridden to be a pleasure at all, even in California which has – in the US context at least – often led the way on circumscribing car use for environmental reasons.

But it is also good to be reminded that the pleasures of the freeway have always been somewhat circumscribed. Banham describes an extraordinarily disciplined environment, in which the freeway freedom is bought at the cost of 'almost total surrender' to the discipline of driving. You can have anything you want so long as you obey the rules, the 'spectacular paradox', as he puts it, of modern capitalism. It is a darker chapter, and a darker book, than is often thought, for the choices it describes are not ours but predetermined ones, and our freedoms illusions. It's a long way from the sunny boosterism of the subsequent film, *Reyner Banham Loves Los Angeles*, in which the freeway is an uncomplicated modern delight. However Banham never entirely resolves the paradox, and you sense his pleasure in its spectacle is tempered with relief that he can, at some point, always go home.

REYNER BANHAM
ECOLOGY IV: AUTOPIA

The first time I saw it happen nothing registered on my conscious mind, because it all seemed so natural – as the car in front turned down the off-ramp of the San Diego freeway, the girl beside the driver pulled down the sun-visor and used the mirror on the back of it to tidy her hair. Only when I had seen a couple more incidents of the kind did I catch their import: that coming off the freeway is coming in from outdoors. A domestic or sociable journey in Los Angeles does not end so much at the door of one's destination as at the off-ramp of the freeway, the mile or two of ground-level streets counts as no more than the front drive of the house.

In part, this is a comment on the sheer vastness of the movement pattern of Los Angeles, but more than that it is an acknowledgement that the freeway system in its totality is now a single comprehensible place, a coherent state of mind, a complete way of life, the fourth ecology of the Angeleno. Though the famous story in *Cry California* magazine about the family who actually lived in a mobile home on the freeways is now known to be a jesting fabrication, the idea was immediately convincing (several other magazines took it seriously and wanted to reprint it) because there was a great psychological truth spoken in the jest. The freeway is where the Angelenos live a large part of their lives.

Such daily sacrifices on the altar of transportation are the common lot of all metropolitan citizens of course. Some, with luck, will spend less time on the average at these devotions, and many will spend them under far more squalid conditions (on the Southern Region of British Railways, or in the New York subway, for instance) but only Los Angeles has made a mystique of such proportions out of its commuting technology that the whole world seems to know about it – tourist postcards from London do not show Piccadilly Circus underground station, but cards from Los Angeles frequently show local equivalents like the 'stack' intersection in downtown; Paris is not famous as the home of the Metro in the way Los Angeles is famous as the home of the Freeway (which must be galling for both Detroit and New York which have better claims, historically). There seem to be two major reasons for their dominance in the city image of Los Angeles and both are aspects of their inescapability; firstly, that they are so vast that you cannot help seeing them, and secondly, that there appears no alternative means of movement and you cannot help using them. There are other and useful streets, and the major boulevards provide an excellent secondary network in many parts of the city, but psychologically, all are felt to be tributary to the freeways.

Furthermore, the actual experience of driving on the freeways prints itself deeply on the conscious mind and unthinking reflexes. As you acquire the special skills involved, the Los Angeles freeways become a special way of being alive, which can be duplicated, in part, on other systems (England would be a much safer place if those skills could be inculcated on our motorways) but not with this totality and extremity. If motorway driving anywhere calls for a high level of attentiveness, the extreme concentration required in Los Angeles seems to bring on a state of heightened awareness that some locals find mystical.

That concentration is required beyond doubt, for the freeways can kill – hardly a week passed but I found myself driving slowly under police control past the wreckage of at least one major crash. But on the other hand the freeways are visibly safe – I never saw any of these incidents, or even minor ones, actually happening, even in weeks where I found I had logged a thousand miles of rush-hour driving. So one learns to proceed with a strange and exhilarating mixture of long-range confidence and close-range wariness. And the freeway system can fail; traffic jams can pile up miles long in rush-hours or even on sunny Sunday afternoons, but these jams are rarely stationary for as long as European expectations would suggest. Really serious jams seem to be about as frequent as hold-ups on London suburban railways, and might – if bad – disrupt the working day of about the same number of citizens, but for most of the time traffic rolls comfortably and driving conditions are not unpleasant. As one habituated to the psychotic driving (as Gerald Priestland has called it) in English cities, and the squalor of the driving conditions, I cannot find it in me to complain about the freeways in Los Angeles; they work uncommonly well.

Angelenos, who have never known anything worse than their local system, find plenty to complain about, and their conversations are peppered with phrases like 'being stuck in a jam in the October heat with the kids in the back puking with the smog'. At first the visitor takes these remarks seriously; they confirm his own most deeply ingrained prejudices about the city that has 'sold its soul to the motor car'. Later, I came to realise that they were little more than standard rhetorical tropes, like English complaints about the weather, with as little foundation in the direct personal experience of the speakers.

This is not to minimise the jams, or even the smog, but both need to be seen in the context of comparisons with other metropolitan areas. On what is regarded as a normally clear day in London, one cannot see as far through the atmosphere as on some officially smoggy days I have experienced in Los Angeles. Furthermore, the photochemical irritants in the smog (caused by the action of sunlight on nitrogen oxides) can be extremely unpleasant indeed in high concentrations, but for the concentration to be high enough to make the corners of my eyes itch painfully is rare in my personal experience, and at no time does the smog contain levels of soot, grit, and corroding sulphur compounds that are still common in the atmospheres of older American and European cities.

It is the psychological impact of smog that matters in Los Angeles. The communal trauma of Black Wednesday (8 September 1943), when the first great smog zapped the city in solid, has left permanent scars, because it broke the legend of the land of eternal sunshine. It was only a legend; the area was never totally pure of atmosphere. The Spaniards called it the Bay of Smokes and could identify it from the ocean by the persistence of smoke from Indian camp-fires, while plots of land in South Cucamonga were advertised in the eighties as being free from 'fog-laden sea-breezes'. But there is a profound psychological difference between fogs caused by Nature's land-forms and light breezes and God-given water, and air-pollution due to the works of man. To make matters worse, analysis showed that a large part of the smog (though not all, one must emphasise) is due to effluents from the automobile. Angelenos were shocked to discover that it was their favourite toy that was fouling up their greatest asset.

But, psychologically shocked or no, most Angeleno freeway-pilots are neither retching with smog nor stuck in a jam; their white-wall tyres are singing over the diamond-cut anti-skid grooves in the concrete road surface, the selector-levers of their automatic gearboxes are firmly in Drive, and the radio is on. And more important than any of this, they are acting out one of the most spectacular paradoxes in the great debate between private freedom and public discipline that pervades every affluent, mechanised urban society.

The private car and the public freeway together provide an ideal – not to say idealised – version of democratic urban transportation: door-to-door movement on demand at high average speeds over a very large area. The degree of freedom and convenience thus offered to all but a small (but now conspicuous) segment of the population is such that no Angeleno will be in a hurry to sacrifice it for the higher efficiency but drastically lowered convenience and freedom of choice of any high-density public rapid-transit system. Yet what seems to be hardly noticed or commented on is that the price of rapid door-to-door transport on demand is the almost total surrender of personal freedom for most of the journey.

The watchful tolerance and almost impeccable lane discipline of Angeleno drivers on the freeways is often noted, but not the fact that both are symptoms of something deeper – willing acquiescence in an incredibly demanding man/machine system. The fact that no single ordinance, specification or instruction manual describes the system in its totality does not make it any less complete or all-embracing – or any less demanding. It demands, first of all, an open but decisive attitude to the placing of the car on the road-surface, a constant stream of decisions that it would be fashionable to describe as 'existential' or even 'situational', but would be better to regard simply as a higher form of pragmatism. The carriage-way is not divided by the kind of kindergarten rule of the road that obtains on British motorways, with their fast, slow, and overtaking lanes (where there are three lanes to use!). The three, four, or five lanes of an Angeleno freeway are virtually equal, the driver is required to select or change lanes according to his speed, surrounding circumstances and future intentions. If everybody does this with the approved mixture of enlightened self-interest and public spirit, it is possible to keep a very large flow of traffic moving quite surprisingly fast.

But at certain points, notably intersections, the lanes are not all equal – some may be pre-empted for a particular exit or change-over ramp as much as a mile before the actual junction. As far as possible the driver must get set up for these pre-empted lanes well in advance, to be sure he is in them in good time because the topology of the intersections is unforgiving. Of course there are occasional clods and strangers who do not sense the urgency of the obligation to set up the lane required good and early, but fortunately they are only occasional (you soon get the message!), otherwise the whole system would snarl up irretrievably. But if these preparations are only an unwritten moral obligation, your actual presence in the correct lane at the intersection is mandatory – the huge signs straddling the freeway to indicate the correct lanes must be obeyed because they are infallible.

At first, these signs can be the most psychologically unsettling of all aspects of the freeway – it seems incredibly bizarre when a sign directs one into the far left lane for an objective clearly visible on the right of the carriageway, but the sign must be believed. No human eye at windscreen level can unravel the complexities of even a relatively simple intersection (none of those in Los Angeles is a symmetrical cloverleaf) fast enough for a normal human brain moving forward at up to sixty mph to make the right decision in time, and there is no alternative to complete surrender of will to the instructions on the signs.

But no permanent system of fixed signs can give warning of transient situations requiring decisions, such as accidents, landslips or other blockages. It is in the nature of a freeway accident that it involves a large number of vehicles, and blocks the carriageway so completely that even emergency vehicles have difficulty in getting to the seat of the trouble, and remedial action such as warnings and diversions may have to be phased back miles before the accident, and are likely to affect traffic moving in the opposite direction in the other carriageway as well. So, inevitably the driver has to rely on other sources of rapid information, and keeps his car radio turned on for warnings of delays and recommended diversions.

Now, the source of these radio messages is not a publicly operated traffic-control radio-transmitter; they are a public service performed by the normal entertainment stations, who

Freeway-scape, drivers' eye view.

derive the information from the police, the Highway Patrol, and their own 'Sigalert' helicopter patrols. Although these channels of information are not provided as a designed component of the freeway system, but arise as an accidental by-product of commercial competition, they are no less essential to the system's proper operation, especially at rush hours. Thus a variety of commanding authorities – moral, governmental, commercial, and mechanical (since most drivers have surrendered control of the transmission to an automatic gearbox) – direct the freeway driver through a situation so closely controlled that, as has been judiciously observed on a number of occasions, he will hardly notice any difference when the freeways are finally fitted with computerised automatic control systems that will take charge of the car at the on-ramp and direct it at properly regulated speeds and correctly selected routes to a preprogrammed choice of off-ramp.

But it seems possible that, given a body of drivers already so well trained, disciplined, and conditioned, realistic cost-benefit analysis might show that the marginal gains in efficiency through automation might be offset by the psychological deprivations caused by destroying the residual illusions of free decision and driving skill surviving in the present situation. However inefficiently organised, the million or so human minds at large on the freeway system at any time comprise a far greater computing capacity than could be built into any machine currently conceivable – why not put that capacity to work by fostering the illusion that it is in charge of the situation?

If illusion plays as large a part in the working of the freeways as it does in other parts of the Angeleno ecology, it is not to be deprecated. The system works as well as it does because the Angelenos believe in it as much as they do; they may squeal when the illusion is temporarily shattered or frustrated; they may share the distrust of the Division of Highways that many liberal souls currently (and understandably) seem to feel; but on leaving the house they still turn the nose of the car towards the nearest freeway ramp because they still believe the freeways are the way to get there. They subscribe, if only covertly, to a deep-seated mystique of freeway driving, and I often suspect that the scarifying stories of the horrors of the freeways are deliberately put about to warn off strangers.

Freeway signs.

Ecology IV: Autopia

Partly this would be to keep inexperienced and therefore dangerous hayseeds off the carriageways, but it would also be to prevent the profanation of their most sacred ritual by the uninitiated. For the Freeway, quite as much as the Beach, is where the Angeleno is most himself, most integrally identified with his great city.

'Say, isn't that your old Aunt Nabby who just passed you in the outer lane of the Berdoo at eighty? There she is, six months in Southern California and already she's got the glued up ash-blond hair, the wrap-around shades and the tight pants and... a chrome yellow Volkswagen with reversed wheels and a voom-voom exhaust.'

Thus wrote Brock Yates in *Car and Driver* magazine, a capsule account of identification with Southern California citizenship via the automobile as a work of art and the freeway as a suitable gallery in which to display it.

The automobile as art-work is almost as specific to the Los Angeles freeways as is the surf-board to the Los Angeles beaches. It has a lengthy tradition behind it, but that tradition drives far less from the imported dream cars, the mile-long Hispanos or the gold Dual-Ghias of the film stars, than from the wonders wrought in backyards by high-school drop-outs upon domestic Detroit-built machines. The art of customising, of turning common family sedans into wild extravaganzas of richly coloured and exotically shaped metal, was delinquent in its origins, however much the present apologists of the hot-rod cult may try to pretend to the contrary, and the drag-racing which is almost the dominant local land-borne sport in Los Angeles is simply a ritualised version of the illegal sprint races that used to take place on the public highways.

But in the uninhibited inventiveness of master customisers like George Barris and Ed Roth, normal straight Los Angeles found something that sprang from the dusty grass roots of its native culture – 'to ride forth seeking romance... to speak in superlatives... to throw dignity out of the window, to dress dramatically... to tackle the impossible' – tamed it, institutionalised it, and applied it in some form to almost every vehicle awheel in the City of Angels (whence its influence has spread back to Detroit and thus to all other motorised parts of the globe). The customised automobile is the natural crowning artefact of the way of life, the human ecology, it adorns.

If you regard the freeways, with Brock Yates, as an 'existential limbo where man sets out each day in search of western-style individualism' then the assertiveness of the style of the art-automobile might be regarded as an aid in that anxious search. But my own observations of Angeleno drivers at close range suggests that many of those who flaunt a wild rail on the Berdoo or the San Mo are relaxed and well-adjusted characters without an identity problem in the world, for whom the freeway is not a limbo of existential angst, but the place where they spend the two calmest and most rewarding hours of their daily lives.

Customised car, George Barris, designer.

Paola Viganò
*The Historian of
the Total Artefact*

//

Reyner Banham
Ecology II: Foothills
Published in *Los Angeles: The Architecture of Four Ecologies*, 1971, pp 94–109.

Paola Viganò
The Historian of the Total Artefact

In 'Ecology II: Foothills' from *Los Angeles: The Architecture of Four Ecologies* (1971) the ambiguity of Banham's position on the theme of ecology emerges. As we know, ecology is a term that was introduced by Ernst Haeckel in the second half of the 19th century, dealing with the way all organisms define their relations with the external world. The term is fundamental in the work of Reyner Banham. However the 'ecology' Banham attends to in *Los Angeles* cannot be considered a pioneer of contemporary understandings of ecological crisis. Banham is, on one hand, attentive to the material modification of the ground, showing a capacity for technical description of the transformation and production of urban space. At the same time, he is fundamentally anchored to an idea of 'human' ecology, far from the attention to the more-than-human environment that characterises attempts to overcome anthropocentric perspectives today.

When Banham explicitly speaks of 'human ecology' in this chapter, we cannot help but go back to the understanding of human ecology held by the Chicago School of the 1920s that extended, in a rather unclear and metaphorical way, concepts belonging to plant and animal life to human communities and dynamics. This use of natural analogies did not make nature its core concern, but rather recognised similarities between human and other animal behaviour and networks in how they experience 'processes of conflict and adjustment'[1]. Borrowing these terms, Banham was certainly aware of their intellectual context, but by the 1970s, the idea of human ecology had taken on different connotations, seen by some geographers as a *futile attempt* to regain something natural. Stronger criticism around growth, environmental devastation and the logic of extraction had risen among American environmentalists of the 1960s, and Los Angeles had come to be seen by many as paradigmatic of this destructive activity. In which vein does Banham therefore speak of ecology in *Los Angeles: The Architecture of Four Ecologies*? As a way to discuss strong biopolitical issues related to population, technology, organisation and environment in Los Angeles? Or as the good engineer that he was – mainly because he was interested in the technical reconfiguration of Los Angeles' ground as a means to make habitable a place that was not easy to settle in? Why *human* ecology?

In fact, making human ecology central is a way for Banham to escape the trap of a narrow and traditional definition of architecture and to enlarge the tools and scope of traditional historians. In *The Architecture of the Well-tempered Environment*, published 1969, Banham makes a case for an understanding of architecture as encompassing a broader range of environmental gestures, writing that 'the history of architecture should cover the whole of the technological art of creating habitable environments', and that 'the traditions of architecture, as we commonly understand the concept, have been forged in societies and cultures that are committed to massively structural methods of environmental management'.[2] This view is expanded in *Los Angeles*, in which ecology paves the way for Banham to present architecture 'within the topographical and historical context of the *total artefact* that constitutes Greater Los Angeles'.[3] Here, human ecology allows a reading of the Los Angeles metropolitan area as 'unprecedented' and 'unrepeatable'; 'neither the prototype of all future cities,' nor, as many planners and environmentalists of the time saw it, 'the harbinger of universal urban doom'.[4] A new interpretation can rise out of this idea: a territory, an entire metropolitan area, as a total artefact. Cities are earthworks, deposits of material culture to be studied by archaeologists, geographers and historians.

Banham shows little regret about the massive mountain-cropping techniques and their ecologically profound consequences in Los Angeles landscapes; a polemic irony even marks his reference to 'the chorus of doom from professional Jeremiahs at Berkeley and in the Sierra Club', whom he is not tempted to join, although he is still obliged to admit that such large-scale interventions into the structure of a region so prone to earthquakes may pose a 'direct physical risk to life and limb'.[5] The principle of reality is more important for the historian of the total artefact than romanticised academic environmental protests: 'short of a social revolution or major economic disaster', the growth on Los Angeles hills would have continued anyway. The total artefact is thus completely depoliticised. The human-made environment extends, in Banham's thought, to the total control of all topographic, atmospheric and technological aspects of our living space. Phrases such as 'man-made weather'[6] produce high fascination in Banham. To be able to create habitable places requires movement towards a system of full environmental control.

The historian of the total artefact reads such a process without moral prejudgment, as an objective archaeological search, inviting close reading and an open-minded understanding of society. The four ecologies were a 'state of mind',[7] suggested Banham's son, Ben, when we met at the Architectural Association in March 2022 on the occasion of Reyner Banham's 100th birthday. It is only too important to maintain this capacity to read the total artefact: even including the updated ecological thinking of the present moment.

It is the only way to acknowledge the complexity of socio-technical, ecological and biopolitical interdependencies. The four (human) ecologies have been the conceptual tool to open our minds to such critical and crucial interpretation.

1   Phil McManus, in *International Encyclopedia of Human Geography*, 2nd edition, edited by Audrey Kobayashi (Elsevier, 2019).
2   Reyner Banham, *The Architecture of the Well-tempered Environment* (Weinberg Modern Books, 1969), p 12; p 20.
3   Emphasis my own. See *Los Angeles: The Architecture of Four Ecologies* (Penguin, 1971), p 23–4.
4   All these quotations are from Reyner Banham, *Los Angeles: The Architecture of Four Ecologies*, p 24.
5   Ibid, p 107; p 109.
6   'The Carrier Corporation, on the other hand, was still using phraseology like "Man-made weather" as late as 1933... Yet the phrase "Man-made weather" is an admirable one ...', Reyner Banham, *The Architecture of the Well-tempered Environment*, p 172.
7   The reference is to Gregory Bateson, *Steps to an Ecology of Mind: Collected Essays in Anthropology, Psychiatry, Evolution, and Epistemology* (University of Chicago Press, 1972).

REYNER BANHAM
ECOLOGY II: FOOTHILLS

Though the original pueblo of Los Angeles was built in the bottomlands of the river valley, the site selected by Governor Felipe de Neve in 1781 is at the last point where the valley narrows, before the Los Angeles River loses itself southward into the plains on the way to the sea. Thus the original settlement could most easily be expanded approximately north and along the river and did so, as the earliest US surveys of the town show, particularly in the creation of the first Mexican 'ghetto' – Sonora Town – to the north. But the customary type of US urban expansion, block by square block in all directions, would obviously engage the grid of streets with the adjoining hill-lands. The extensions proposed in Lieutenant Ord's survey of 1849 sensibly stay on the flattish valley-bottom, but civilians cannot be relied on to go where the military direct them and the city was soon engaged with the small hills to east and west, and was building on their tops by the 1880s.

The characteristic townscape created in the process has almost entirely vanished – though the steeply-terraced rooming houses on either side of the Angel's Flight funicular railway will be lovingly recalled by all fanciers of old private-detective movies. But that old high density development of the hillsides belonged to a primarily pedestrian concept of cities and their workings; they were but a tiny – if likeable – segment within a city whose conception of itself was neither figuratively nor physically pedestrian. All that Bunker Hill and the steeper parts of Boyle Heights had in common with the Los Angeles we know were the problems of footings and foundations on steep slopes made of little more than compacted sand.

By the middle seventies an alternative kind of hill country was being brought within sight of development – a kind of development that was to become highly typical of the area and pretty well unlike anything else in the world. Although the Santa Monica railway line was careful to run economically across the flat lands on its way to the sea, it had the lower slopes of the Hollywood Hills and the Santa Monica mountain handily to its north for almost its entire length, and it is upon that mountain that the classic Los Angeles foothill settlements were to appear.

Already in the eighties attempts were made to create cities between the mountain and the railroad. On the Wolfskill Ranch, in the tumbled lands where the present Wilshire Boulevard begins to turn south after Beverly Glen, was founded the city of Sunset – from that point of vantage it might just have been possible to see the sun setting over the ocean beyond Santa Monica. In 1880 the inevitable resort hotel was built and land pegged out – and nothing happened and not a trace of it has been seen since. Further east, about where Cañon Drive now runs, another city, called Morocco, was laid out in 1888, and again seems to have vanished without trace. The full development of even these eminently desirable lands would have to wait, like so many other things in Los Angeles, for the electric trains, and these arrived with the Pasadena and Pacific lines of Sherman and Clark in 1895.

The classic spread of residential foothills now runs, westward in geographical order but not sequence of development, from Silverlake (built around the reservoir of that name), through Los Feliz (for want of a better name), Hollywood, West Hollywood, Beverly Hills, Bel Air, Brentwood, and Pacific Palisades where the foothills fall into the Pacific (literally so, after heavy rainstorms!). Eastward from the Los Angeles River, the sequence runs: Highland Park, Pasadena, San Marino to the south, Sierra Madre, and then they begin to tail off with decreasing conviction through Monrovia. This decrease of conviction stems from a basic socio-economic consideration which becomes stunningly apparent on any map that shows the distribution of average incomes; the financial and topographical contours correspond almost exactly: the higher the ground the higher the income. But – and this is where Los Angeles lines up with other cities for once – who ever heard of any rich suburbs much to the east of any downtown?

But south, of course, is a traditional area for superior suburbs in any city, and Los Angeles is no exception. The larger southerly enclave is on Palos Verdes mountain, whose inherently desirable landscape of broken grassland and planted woods with views over the sea contains the tremendously superior settlements of Palos Verdes, Palos Verdes Estates, Rolling Hills, and Rolling Hills Estates. The smaller southern enclave is an oddity; Baldwin Hills is an area of unlovely scrub largely given over to the oil industry, cross-country motorcycling, or just waste, topped by a concrete reservoir that burst one memorable night in 1912 and is still dry. But on the north face (wrong, for a start; foothill settlements typically face south) and round to the east, is a perfectly typical foothill development complete with tortuous roads and restrictive covenants in the title deeds which exclude Negroes and Mexicans. And at the foot of the slope is the rather untypical Baldwin Hills Village, a textbook example of a Radburn-planned superblock. Planning in any normal sense is not too common in Los Angeles (though there is more than might be expected) but its greatest example in the area is another foothill city, Beverly Hills.

As an example, Beverly Hills is almost too good; the regular pattern of lightly curving roads running north-west from Santa Monica Boulevard, maintaining approximate symmetry about the double axis of Cañon and Beverly Drives, which cross when they intersect Sunset Boulevard, exchanging position in order to create the triangular site for the Beverly Hills Hotel... that's all just drawing-board geometry, capable of absorbing the gentle rise in the land surface from Boulevard to Boulevard, but incapable of extension back into the broken country behind, where the pretty diagram begins to lose its symmetry and the streets rapidly abandon all pretence to geometrical order and become little more than black-topped mountain trails.

That is what the foothill ecology is really all about: narrow, tortuous residential roads serving precipitous house-plots that often back up directly on unimproved wilderness even now; an air of deeply buried privacy even in relatively broad valley-bottoms in Stone Canyon or Mandeville Canyon. Even more than the second-growth woodlands of Connecticut or the heathlands of the Kentish Charts, this is landscape that seems to cry out for affluent suburban residences, and to flourish when so employed. Watered, it will carry almost any kind of vegetation that horticultural fantasy might conceive. Indeed, there is no native style of gardening in common practice at all, and cacti and other desert plants are quite difficult to find in the foothill cities. What are not difficult to find are laurels and other dense-growing small-leaved shrubs that can be used to make thickets of instant privacy, essential to the fat life of the delectable mountains.

Angel's Flight funicular railway, 1901.

Townscape in Bel Air.

The fat life is well known around the world, wherever television re-runs old movies on the Late Show or its local equivalent; it is the life, factual and fictional, of Hollywood's classic years. The outward show of this style is seen – with increasing difficulty through the occluding boscage – by the increasingly elderly patronage of the bus tours of Famous Film Stars' Homes; the inner workings of the style were as essential to the private detective movies as was the townscape of downtown – where would the private eyes of the forties have been without laurel shrubberies to lurk in, sweeping front drives to turn the car in, terraces from which to observe the garden below, massive Spanish Colonial Revival doors on which to knock, and tiled Spanish Colonial Revival interiors for the knocking to echo in, and the bars of Spanish Colonial Revival windows to hold on, or rambling split-level ranch house plans in which to lose the opposition, and random rubble fireplace walls to pin suspects against, and gigantic dream-bedrooms from which the sun may be seen rising in heartbreaking picture-postcard splendour over the Hollywood Hills... and the essential swimming pool for the bodies.

It was in this kind of residential landscape that the very real Bugsy Siegel was rubbed out; the world of the private eye was fact, and much of that fact survives. Visiting houses in Beverly Hills or Bel Air can be an hallucinating experience; an overwhelming sense of déjà vu mingles with an overwhelming desire to sidle along corridors with one's back to the wall and to kick doors wide open before passing through. The same urges seem not to be felt (by myself, at least) in the beach-houses of Malibu, however many movies they may have appeared in, which suggests that there is a peculiar authority about the Beverly Hills type of human ecology when seen and transmitted through the eyes of Hollywood – and so there should be; Hollywood Boulevard is the main street of the foothills, and Beverly Hills is where Hollywood lived from the time Douglas Fairbanks and Mary Pickford gave it the seal of approval by buying their piece of land on Summit Drive.

The sense of departed glory in those foothills is strong, but the built and planted structure remains almost untouched – this is still an immensely desirable human ecology for those who can afford it, and not just in Beverly Hills. The Rolls-Royces are still outside the door of the Blacker house in

Beverly Hills looking north in 1922. From the Spence Collection, courtesy of The Benjamin and Gladys Thomas Air Photo Archives at the UCLA Geography Department.

Pasadena and the Ferraris still negotiate the twisting roads of Palos Verdes as to the manner born, the Continentals turn in the forecourt of the Bel Air Hotel – and well-bred hooves still clatter in Mandeville Canyon. In so far as this ecology is threatened it is by its own desirability more than anything else; a desirability attested by the appearance of small two or three-storey apartment blocks balanced awkwardly over impossibly precipitous pocket handkerchief sites on the back lanes of Beverly Glen, and other areas beyond the zones developed by larger houses in the more accessible foothills.

    They are one of the signs that this kind of domestic ecology is coming to an inevitable end. As back-lane development testifies, accessible and buildable sites are becoming more and more rare, and few old ones have yet been liberated for redevelopment. More than this, steep foothill sites demand a building technology that is out of step with what is increasingly normal in Los Angeles today. Whether it is the crudest dingbat or something much more sophisticated, the Angeleno house of the sixties has tended to be the house of a plainsman, not a mountaineer. The economics of its structural technology imply a flat building-surface, not a sloping one; and those economics are demanding enough to ensure that the site will be a flat one by some means or other.

Beverly Hills looking north in 1952. From the Spence Collection, courtesy of The Benjamin and Gladys Thomas Air Photo Archives at the UCLA Geography Department.

The common solution for a long time has been to create a framed substructure of some sort, with supporting posts and tiles and 'deadmen' to fix it back to the slope behind and stop the whole affair sliding. Craig Ellwood's Smith house on Crestwood Drive is a classic of this kind of solution, because the flat-floored single-storeyed house is integrated with the supporting frame below, a common steel structure continuing the bay-system of his customary glass-box aesthetic down to the footings on the slope and leaving the space underneath wide open. A more or less equivalent solution in wood, integrating the sub-frame with the architecture above, can be seen in the Seidenbaum house off Mulholland Drive, designed by Richard Dorman, and much of the supposed eccentricity of the domestic architecture of John Lautner is traceable to the attempt to solve this kind of problem – his famous Chemosphere house (also off Mulholland) standing on its single concrete column is a very reasonable and well worked out solution, given the forty-five degree slope of the site. Alternatively, the un-thought-out solution – if solution it is – simply takes a standard developer's tract-house and perches it in mid-air on steel uprights, a surreal image of plainsmen's houses apparently airborne and detached from earth which can be seen to good (or ludicrous) effect on the San Fernando side of Coldwater Canyon, in Laurel Canyon, and elsewhere.

However, the classic intrusions of plainsmen's housing into foothill ecology depend on a fundamentally different way of making the building surface flat – scraping away the mountain until you have enough horizontal surface, not to create merely a levelled terrace in front of a house but to create a street-sized terrace to carry a dozen or more houses, or a plateau big enough to carry a whole tract. Given the basically sandy structure of the hills, and the sophistication of modern bulldozing, scraping, and grading equipment, mountains of this kind can be moved without much sweat, albeit plenty of noise and dust. Indeed, the greatest of all the monuments of the foothills is just such an earth-form (though basically a natural one), the Hollywood Bowl, home of the famous open-air concerts. But 'mountain cropping' is not concerned with creating monuments of the earthmover's art; just using earth-moving techniques to create an environment where current tract-house building technology can operate by its normal flatland habits. And this, apparently, is still the most economical way of building in the foothills; architect-proposed alternatives, such as cutting the price of sub-frames by mass-producing their component parts seem to be non-starters – for years a system of standardised subframes covering a slope below Sunset Mesa stood abandoned with no houses on it, and only a few have been built on it even now.

The effects of mountain-cropping techniques are obviously going to be profound, ecologically and otherwise. Without joining the chorus of doom from professional Jeremiahs at Berkeley and in the Sierra Club, I must still admit that it proposes a different kind of ecological disturbance to those previously practised in Los Angeles. Though, obviously, all building in foothill territory must involve some disturbance of the soil, the customary methods of working and designing did not alter the profiles of whole hills, exalt valleys, or make waste places plain, in the way that large-scale mountain cropping does. Indeed, the wholesale planting probably helped to stabilise the land forms by thickening the root-mat and delaying water run-off. The existing and famous slide areas, which have provided literary minds with a ready-made metaphor of the alleged moral decay of Los Angeles, are

Smith house, West Los Angeles, 1955, Craig Ellwood, architect.

Seidenbaum house, Mulholland Drive, Richard Dorman, architect.

House-frames, Sunset Mesa.

Hollywood Bowl, before alterations of 1969, architectural design, Lloyd Wright.

Ecology II: Foothills

Chemosphere house, Hollywood Hills, 1960, John Lautner, architect.

usually associated with under-cutting rather than summit cropping – existing flat areas at the foot of sand cliffs have been cut into for road widening, or enlarging parking lots. This in itself may not increase the steepness of the slope beyond a seemingly safe angle of repose, but building, planting, etc higher up the hill may have produced changes in drainage patterns sufficient to unsettle the whole bluff, and thus produce continuously crumbling cliffs like that above the Pacific Coast Highway at Chatauqua. This has produced at least one major fall a month whenever I have been staying in Los Angeles.

Whether the existing codes governing grading and filling work, which date only from 1952 in the city, and 1957 in the county, will be adequate for large-scale cropping remains to be seen – after the storms of 1969 I have my own doubts. Really big cropping like that at the top of Topanga Canyon involves cutting deep into the underlying geology, and totally filling ravines and other drainage runs, so it becomes difficult not to entertain apocalyptic queries about how some of these developments are going to settle down – and where! Such large-scale triflings with the none-too-stable structure of an area of high earthquake risk seems more portentous as a direct physical risk to life and limb than as a lost ecological amenity. Naturally one regrets the disappearance of Southern California's attractively half-tamed wildernesses, but short of a social revolution or major economic disaster they were going to get built on anyhow. The worry is that these extensive human settlements have been constructed on sands that have been shifted once by an outside agency, and may decide to shift for themselves at any time.

However, mountain cropping on this scale is currently restricted to the fringes of the Los Angeles area, and is nowhere yet on the cataclysmic scale of the reworked topographies further north – the most spectacular examples in *How to Kill a Golden State* by William Bronson (to whom I am indebted for the phrase 'mountain cropping') nearly all seem to be in San Mateo county, outside San Francisco and handily adjacent to the notorious San Andreas Fault. In the Los Angeles area the demand for hill-lands is not yet so acute; in the San Fernando Valley, in Orange County and on the fringes of the desert beyond the mountains there is land yet, accessible from the freeways, where the eternal plainsmen can settle and build for pleasure and, above all, for profit. While this persists, and the zoning ordinances are not too often waived, the original residential foothills can expect to remain mostly undisturbed, embosked ever deeper in their tortuous roads and laurel privacies, epitomes of the great middle-class suburban dream.

Curt Gambetta
I Was There

//

Reyner Banham
Introduction

Published in *A Concrete Atlantis: U.S. Industrial Buildings* and *European Modern Architecture*, 1986, pp 1–21.

Curt Gambetta
I Was There

Banham envisaged an assertive, guiding role for the historian in the production of architectural knowledge from early on in his career. In the essay 'History and Psychiatry' (1960), for example, Banham argued that the historian should 'plot the course' for the architectural discipline, knowing full well that the historian's search for truth might embarrass the modern movement with inconvenient historical facts about its origins. To earn the trust of architects, the historian would need to operate outside of the architectural field – this was the only 'secure ground' for the historian to stand on. According to Banham, architects increasingly looked to historians to help them answer existential questions such as 'How did I get this way?', forcing historians to be veritable psychiatrists and guardians of the profession's 'conscience'. The amateur historian, whom Banham described as 'the historian with architectural connections', was too compromised to bear such a responsibility.[1]

Despite his reservations about their work, Banham held space for the amateur historian's contributions. Describing their efforts as fieldwork and comparing it to the labour of prospectors and surveyors, Banham portrayed a lively scene of 'enthusiasts' and 'self-appointed commandos' in search of early houses by André Lurçat and interiors by Frank Lloyd Wright. Banham cautioned professional historians against determining the amateur's journeys in advance, lest they overburden their unpredictable itineraries with preconceptions. Still, much as early anthropologists interpreted facts gathered by others in the field, Banham claimed historical interpretation as the proper domain of the professional historian. Though he acknowledged a coterie of amateur fieldworkers who had fanned out across Europe and the US in search of lesser modernist works, Banham cautioned that the historian should produce the 'final map' that results from their fieldwork. Paternalistically, he saw fieldworkers as needing the 'authority of a trained professional mind' and someone that they can trust – in other words, the historian.[2]

Decades later, in the introduction to *A Concrete Atlantis: U.S. Industrial Building and European Modern Architecture* (1986), Banham assumed the role of fieldworker.[3] He suggested right in the opening passage that his firsthand narration of American industrial buildings will be different from other elements of his story. His evocative descriptions of industrial buildings were to constitute the 'observational parts' of the book, or his 'fieldwork'. But one might ask whether the other fragments of evidence in the introduction – semi-fictional accounts, a partial photographic image, and faulty memories of a series of industrial boilers and adjacent open concrete frame on Cannery Row in Santa Cruz, California – were not also a kind of fieldwork. Banham assembled them all into a field of knowledge about industrial architecture, juxtaposing historical fragments and literary narrative with firsthand observations. This was in keeping with histories of fieldwork in other domains. As James Clifford, Banham's colleague at UC Santa Cruz, has observed, anthropological field notes teemed with marginalia and different points of view that included transcriptions, real-time fragments of experience and personal experiences written down later, that resulted in a polyphonic text.[4] Like the anthropologist's field notebook, *A Concrete Atlantis* reckoned with a multitude of voices, personal memories and fragments from the history of architecture.

It is Banham's voice, however, that resonated most strongly. He set aside the distanced objectivity of third-person narration in favor of a first-person narrative, as if to say: 'I was there'. *A Concrete Atlantis* is, in this respect, a eulogy to antiquarian fieldwork, the authority of which relied on first-person narrative and staged depictions of the antiquarian savant at work in ruins and volcanic landscapes – often those of Europe's southern extremities.[5] Never mind that antiquarian fieldwork was an ineluctably collaborative endeavour involving myriad local fieldworkers and varied expertise. Similarly, *A Concrete Atlantis* was a collective work, researched and conceived with colleagues and students in multiple times and places, as the acknowledgements at the beginning of the book make clear.[6]

Though Banham's narration smoothed over the craggy polyphony of their research, it dramatised other aspects of the book's making. Accompanied by photographs, quotations and fragments of architectural history, descriptions of fieldwork in Santa Cruz, Buffalo and northwest Germany demonstrated how historical evidence is produced and interpreted as it circulates between different technological mediums and interpretive communities. Banham was not a bystander to such an undertaking. Whether in Cannery Row or the grain elevators of Buffalo, Banham placed himself in the vantage points of historical texts and images. Using new photographs and thick, firsthand description, Banham noted blind spots and contributed new evidence and analysis for consideration. In this way, fieldwork narratives registered his participation in the production and interpretation of historical evidence.[7]

Because *A Concrete Atlantis* is focused on Banham's voice and experiences, the interpretive lens of his collaborators did not find expression, with the exception of several student-made drawings and photographs taken by Patricia Layman Bazelon and historian Jack Quinan.[8] In a manner akin to the relationship between anthropologist and native informant, the book's production relied on a division of labour between local observers (eg students, faculty, historians and photographers who were from the region, in addition to Banham himself) and participants in a field of knowledge (eg Banham, a professional historian). However, historical research shows that their inquiries assumed other forms, apart from Banham's single authored text.[9] With Banham's support, students and professors in Buffalo created other venues for historical research by founding a new degree programme and completing an exhibition based on their fieldwork in 1977. As architectural history reckons with longstanding biases and blind spots, their efforts challenge us to revisit a question that Banham first asked early in his career, and which the production of *A Concrete Atlantis* raised anew: who participates in the making of architectural history?

1   Banham clarifies that the historian must assure the accuracy of any 'journey', but not presuppose its destinations: 'Without the ballast of an equivalent millennial tradition, architecture will have to be consciously trimmed and steered as it proceeds, and someone will have to plot its course continually. That someone is the historian: it is not for him to give orders or indicate destinations, but his plot of the track to date must be accurate.' Reyner Banham, 'History and Psychiatry', in *Design By Choice*, edited by Penny Sparke (Rizzoli, 1981), p 22.
2   Ibid.
3   A role and narrative form that was instrumental to Banham's other writings, especially *Scenes in America Deserta* (Gibbs M Smith and Thames and Hudson, 1982).
4   James Clifford, 'Notes on (Field)notes', in *Fieldnotes: The Makings of Anthropology*, edited by Roger Sanjek (Cornell University Press, 1990), pp 47–70. Others have noted that field notebooks also included sketches, ruminations on fiction and other scholarly works, and myriad other fragments of cogitation and lived experience. See Michael Taussig, *I Swear I Saw This: Drawings in Fieldwork Notebooks, Namely My Own* (University of Chicago Press, 2011).
5   I am grateful to Hadas Steiner for relating Banham's approach to fieldwork to earlier histories of field science, including early 20th century efforts to move beyond antiquarian models of research and narration. See Hadas Steiner, 'Banham at 100', a paper presented at *What Happens on your 100th Birthday? A Set of Confabulations in Memory of Peter Reyner Banham*, a symposium at the AA, London, 4 March 2022.
6   This included extensive collaboration with the State University of New York at Buffalo faculty member and architect Beverly 'Bonnie' Foit-Albert.
7   On Banham's participation in the production of architectural history, see Hadas Steiner, 'Cropping the View: Reyner Banham and the Image of Buffalo', in *Buffalo at the Crossroads: The Past, Present, and Future of American Urbanism*, edited by Peter H Christensen (Cornell University Press, 2020), pp 255–64.
8   New photographs included in the book were taken by Banham, the professional photographer Patricia Layman Bazelon and historian Jack Quinan.
9   See Curt Gambetta and Hadas Steiner, 'Field Observations', in *Radical Pedagogies*, edited by Beatriz Colomina et al (MIT Press, 2022), pp 190–2.

REYNER BANHAM
INTRODUCTION TO A CONCRETE ATLANTIS

This inquiry into the connections between North American industrial building and the classic modernist architecture of the International Style in Europe must cover many locations and publications on both sides of the Atlantic and might make its point of departure almost anywhere within its time span of 1900–1925; but the juncture at which its main currents seemed to spark together most enlighteningly in my own eyes was not in the presence of some monumental structure or provocative text, but among the abandoned onshore installations of the defunct sardine fisheries of Monterey Bay in California, almost the only point where this narrative intersects the main traditions of Western literature. In his picaresque novel *Cannery Row*, John Steinbeck, needing to explain a part of the tale's setting, gives a very plausible account of the disposal of some obsolete industrial equipment:

'In April 1932 the boiler at the Hediondo Cannery blew a tube for the third time in two weeks and the board of directors consisting of Mr Randolph and a stenographer decided that it would be cheaper to buy a new boiler than to have to shut down so often. In time the new boiler arrived and the old one was moved into the vacant lot between Lee Chang's and the Bear Flag Restaurant, where it was set up on blocks... The boiler looked like an old-fashioned locomotive without wheels. It had a big door in the centre of its nose, and a low fire-door... Below the boiler on the hill there were a number of large pipes also abandoned by the Hediondo.'[1]

This makes an apt point at which to begin this study, not only because so much of the book will be about the abandoned installations of American industry – they are the preponderant subject of what might be called the observational parts, or fieldwork – or because the eyes that did the observing were my European ones, though this study is fundamentally concerned with European views of American industry, but also because of what occurred when I first started to visit Cannery Row in Monterey in the early 1980s.

In those days before the recent drastic 'gentrifications', old-timers along the Row would still point out to unsuspecting tourists what they claimed were the original Hediondo 'boilers and the big pipes where the hoboes used to sleep'. The claim was false, however; the location did not tally with that clearly established in Steinbeck's text, any more than does the site of the present 'boiler' that has been installed for the benefit of the organised tourist trade. More than that, Steinbeck also speaks of a single horizontal boiler, whereas what stood on this falsely identified site at the end of the Row were three tall, fat, crusty-black vertical cylinders that had probably once been oil tanks. Next to them, however – and this was what made the site so intriguing to me – was an apparently unfinished concrete structure, a flat, square ground-slab carrying one storey-height of vertical square columns whose heads were joined by equally simple square concrete beams.[2] This was not great architecture, in the sense that many of the concrete-framed industrial buildings to be discussed later in this book are undoubtedly great by the standards of any period. Indeed it was barely architecture at all; it was like the merest diagram of an idealised reinforced concrete-frame structure, the sort of thing that used to appear in worthy books claiming to instruct lay-people in the fundamental principles of modern architecture, an image as familiar as any of the other older furniture of my mind.

But, looking through the open spaces defined by its square members to the closed bulks of the cylinders behind, I seemed to be seeing something else, equally familiar, but not observed in so perfectly abstracted a form before: the very essentials; the 'ultimate metaphysic of form' of the high period of the International Style around 1930, as summed up in the 'Two Geometries' of Le Corbusier; the 'dialectical confrontation between sculptural forms and gridded space' of which Richard Etlin has spoken[3] and which I suggest is a European derivative of the closed forms of American industrial storage containers and of the openly gridded loft space of regular American factories.

This book will argue that there is a causal, cultural, and conscious connection between such masterworks of explicit architectural modernism as the Cite de Refuge or the Villa Savoye and the utilitarian structures of a certain period and type of North American industry. The existence of such a connection and its apparently deliberate nature have been noted from time to time in the literature of twentieth-century architecture. For instance, the authors of *Learning from Las Vegas* have observed:

'The architecture of the Modern movement, during its early decades and through a number of its masters, developed a vocabulary of forms based on a variety of industrial models whose conventions and proportions were no less explicit than the Classical orders of the Renaissance. What Mies did with linear industrial buildings in the 1940s, Le Corbusier had done with plastic grain elevators in the 1920s, and Gropius had done with the Bauhaus in the 1930s (sic), imitating his own earlier factory, the Faguswerk of 1911. Their factorylike buildings were more than 'influenced' by the industrial vernacular structures of the then recent past, in the sense that historians have described influences among artists and movements. Their buildings were explicitly adapted from these sources, and largely for their symbolic content, because industrial structures represented, for European architects, the brave new world of science and technology...

Le Corbusier among the Modern masters was unique in elaborately describing industrial prototypes for his architecture in *Vers une Architecture*. However, even he claimed the steamship and the grain elevator for their forms rather than their associations, for their simple geometry rather than their industrial image. It is significant, on the other hand, that the buildings of Le Corbusier, illustrated in his book, physically resemble the steamships and the grain elevators but not the Parthenon or the furniture in Santa Maria in Cosmedin and Michelangelo's details for Saint Peter's, which are also illustrated for their simple geometric forms. The industrial prototypes became literal models for Modern architecture, while the historical-architectural prototypes were merely analogues selected for certain of their characteristics. To put it another way, the industrial buildings were the right style; the historical buildings were not.'[4]

Grain silo and elevator, Fort William.

This was well observed (if somewhat self-contradictory and poorly argued), and the fundamental truth of its observations could be confirmed in almost daily confrontations and comparisons at any time after the International Style became the established mode for new constructions in North America. For a period at the end of the 1970s, for instance, one could look out over downtown Providence, Rhode Island, from the raised platforms of the train station and see the façade of a new multi-storey hotel visually superimposed on that of an old, 1920s multi-storey factory behind it – and the two façades were almost identical cellular grids of concrete structural members! Their dimensions and expression seemed the same, yet one had been built some forty years earlier than the other and for an entirely different stated function.

Now, one must acknowledge that there are accepted explanations for such resemblances that do not involve conscious emulation of forms. Many Marxist historians, as well as the kind of rationalist who used to offer the standard justifications for 'modern architecture', would probably propose that the economic rationalities of society at those times would make that particular form of construction, with its necessary floor heights and structurally optimised bay widths between columns, the only conceivable mode of building those structures, irrespective of their overt functions, since both were in practice conceived as little more than profitably rentable bulk floor space.

Such explanations may not be set aside; buildings in the 'real world' are built for real-world reasons and will show the effects of those reasons and the world views that support them. Yet such explanations have nothing to say about the fact that profitably rentable hotel space of the same period as that factory did not exhibit its concrete frame in this way, but concealed it behind a garment of brick and stone in whatever period style was thought appropriate by architect and client. These simple economic explanations are not only too glib to explain what happened in detail, but also tend to look pitifully inadequate and subhuman when measured against the views and expressed responses of those 'masters' whom *Learning from Las Vegas* credits with having imposed an industrial aesthetic on their architecture – Walter Gropius comparing American industrial buildings to the 'work of the ancient Egyptians' in their overwhelming monumentality,[5] or Le Corbusier announcing that 'The American engineers overwhelm with their calculations our expiring architecture,'[6] or Erich Mendelsohn in 1924 writing to his wife in Berlin after his visit to Buffalo, New York:

'Mountainous silos, incredibly space-conscious, but creating space. A random confusion amidst the chaos of loading and unloading of corn ships, of railways and bridges, crane monsters with live gestures, hordes of silo cells in concrete, stone and glazed brick. Then suddenly a silo with administrative buildings, closed horizontal fronts against the stupendous verticals of fifty to a hundred cylinders, and all this in the sharp evening light. I took photographs like mad. Everything else so far now seemed to have been shaped interim to my silo dreams. Everything else was merely a beginning.'[7]

This kind of rhetoric seems to open up totally different types of historical questions, about the 'why and wherefore' of the adoption of this industrial aesthetic, but these matters have been very little discussed in the literature so far. During the four decades when the International Style was the dominant architectural mode, such matters probably could not have been discussed at all. In the eyes of the great historians-apologists of the style, like Giedion and Pevsner, there would be little point in discussing what was a self-evident historical necessity. For them the International Style was not only the true style of the early twentieth century, as the Baroque had been of the late seventeenth, but was also a true style in the sense that, far from being copied from any previous epoch, it had arisen out of structural and constructional necessity, out of the service of the manifest needs of man and society, as the High Gothic of the thirteenth century was supposed to have done.

For that generation, the rationalist type of explanation was enough – or very nearly so. If the Bauhaus building looked like the Fagus factory, or the façades of Le Corbusier's *rues à Redents* looked somewhat like the elevations of Ford's Model-T plant at Highland Park, it was because all of these buildings were honest expressions of the functional needs of their users or inhabitants. At no time, one must suspect, was this kind of rhetoric believed absolutely; if Louis Sullivan's proposition that 'form follows function' had been pursued objectively and resolutely, there would be no way in which a design school could look like a factory, or an apartment block in Paris could resemble an automobile plant in the Detroit suburbs. These doctrines and dictums, it now seems clear, were sincerely believed and honestly applied, but at the level of symbolism or (perhaps more accurately) as a form of allegory.

The appearance of industrial resemblances in nonindustrial buildings was construed, rather, as a *promise* that these buildings would be as functionally honest, structurally economical and, above all, as up-to-the-minute as any of the American factories that Le Corbusier hailed as 'the first fruits of the New Age'[8]. The forms of factories and grain elevators were an available iconography, a language of forms, whereby promises could be made, adherence to the modernist credo could be asserted, and the way pointed to some kind of technological utopia.

The word *utopia* is used advisedly but in a specialised sense here: it has become a commonplace that utopian dreams, utopian claims, utopian projects infest the architecture of the early years of the twentieth century and that modern technology was to play a large part in most of them. In this case, however, the utopia in view was not imaginary, improbable, nor located in the distant future. The industrial buildings of North America were distant from the younger European modernists only in mileage and were not imaginary; they had concrete – literally concrete – presence here on earth. European modernists may well have needed to make powerful imaginative leaps in order to comprehend what they believed to be happening in North America, and the views they expressed may have been flavoured by their own wishful imaginings, but unlike other utopians they could point to an apparently ideal state of affairs that actually existed in their own time. That is why I have chosen to call it an *Atlantis* rather than a *utopia*, taking my cue from Francis Bacon's *New Atlantis*, in which he describes an island in the ocean some long way to the west of Europe and specifically compares it to 'the Great Atlantis (that you call America)', though only to differentiate the real place from the imaginary.[9]

However, Bacon's Atlantis suggests even richer comparisons with what was happening in the minds of European modernists who turned to American industrial architecture for inspiration. His *New Atlantis* was a society transformed by the application of scientific method, but on almost every page of the text one is made aware of the extent to which its continued functioning was governed by the persistence of rules of conduct based on Christian charity and Christian grace. The idealised but concrete industrial architecture of North America, the product of a strict and modern engineering rationalism derived from the kind of scientific methodology proposed by Bacon, was also discovered to contain the perennial and absolute virtues of an earlier architectural tradition: Le Corbusier believed that the work of these engineers rang 'in unison with universal order',[10] while Walter Gropius more pointedly supposed that 'American builders have preserved a natural feeling for large compact forms fresh and intact.'[11]

One may find these views naïve, but they contain concepts and understandings shot through with the cultural contradictions of the world of architecture in the first decades of the present century: that simultaneous quest for pure modernity and also ancient certainty that informs the works, and above all the writings, of Adolf Loos, for example. Loos was also one of the key figures in establishing the period's pervasive myths of the clean modernity of America.[12] In the context of European understandings of industrial architecture, however, these generalised ideas take on a sharper point. America was not only the land of the future, as generations of hopeful Europeans had supposed, but was also – and here again it is Gropius who produces the telling phrase – the *Mutterland der Industrie*.

If the interests and researches of that generation had been more rational and less romantic, the European modernists could have found nearly all the virtues and architectural forms they admired in America among the works of their direct European predecessors; indeed many of the American concrete structures they celebrated would have been impossible without the patented processes and the built examples of European engineers. But America had an overwhelming and legendary prestige for modernity – and many of the European engineers would be compromised, in the eyes of younger, radical architects, by their association with established architects of the older, unreformed and nonmodern generation. Even so, it seems to be true in the end that it was only some kind of chapter of fortunate accidents in architectural patronage and periodical publication that finally gave America the special status of the Concrete Atlantis.

Architecture remains a predominantly visual art; this may be regrettable but it is a historical and cultural fact, and it means that architects are educated and influenced primarily by the force of visual example. What were the most fundamental examples for this particular group is abundantly clear: seven pages of almost unexplained illustrations of American grain elevators and factories that appeared as an insert in the *Jarhbuch des Deutschen Werkbundes* for 1913. These illustrations immediately followed an important introductory article by the Werkbund's president Friedrich Naumann[13] and were thus also the first illustrations seen by the reader. But they belonged to the following article, '*Die Entwicklung Moderner Industriebaukunst*,' by Walter Gropius, who had been soliciting these pictures from various sources in America and Canada for over a year during the preparation of the article. What had specifically turned his attention to American industrial building, however, cannot have been direct experience, since he was not to cross the Atlantic until after he left the Bauhaus in 1928. It must have been his connections with the Benscheidt family in Hannover and Alfeld, who were his clients on the Fagus factory. They had seen American plants in 1910 during their meetings with the United Shoe Machinery Company in Beverly, Massachusetts, the firm who was the prime investor in the Fagus concern and whose Beverly factory, designed by the great concrete 'pioneer' Ernest L Ransome, was a model demonstration structure in the most up-to-date mode.

The impact of these illustrations, however, was felt throughout 'modern Europe' and registered as early as 1914 in the work of Antonio Sant'Elia and Mario Chiattone, the architect members of the Futurist circle in Italy, and even more strikingly in the sketchbooks and imaginary projects of Erich Mendelsohn – these indeed were the preliminary outlines of the 'silo dreams' that were realised before his eyes in Buffalo in 1924. In 1919 Le Corbusier (who was not to set foot in any America for another sixteen years) wrote to Gropius asking to borrow the grain elevator illustrations for use in the magazine *L'Esprit Nouveau*,[14] and a year later one of them appeared

Concrete frame and abandoned tanks. Cannery Row, Monterey, California.

Washburn-Crosby Elevator, Buffalo.

in an article by Erich Mendelsohn. By 1927, when two of Gropius' illustrations appeared in *Der Sieg des Neuen Baustils* by Walter Curt Behrendt,[15] they had already become almost commonplace, having been seen worldwide in the book *Vers une Architecture*, which Le Corbusier assembled out of those earlier magazine articles. From then on, they were established icons of modernity and architectural probity. Their last appearance without satire or historicising commentary was, as far as one can tell, in Vincent Scully's *American Architecture and Urbanism* in 1969.[16]

How could fourteen illustrations, only moderately well reproduced from other publications, ever attain such commanding and durable power? For a start, the practitioners of the International Style – then innocently known as just 'modern architecture' – needed objective confirmation of their formal preferences. Believing itself to be the very antithesis of a revived or invented style, the movement had to take a stand somewhere outside the 'fevered imaginations of architects' or the supposedly hot-house atmosphere of the academies. 'Let us believe the words of American engineers,' said Le Corbusier, 'but let us beware of American architects!'[17] This command will need further attention in the last section of this book, but here it serves to indicate a state of mind that sought architectural virtue by going outside the privileged circles of professional architecture as then understood, much as previous generations with similar problems had turned to the vernacular buildings of peasants and primitives in search of honest constructions and clear expressions of function.

In an age when pretensions of peasant primitivism were becoming increasingly difficult for a sophisticated person to sustain (if only because peasant standards of personal hygiene were no longer tolerable to sensitive souls in Europe), works of engineering were happily co-opted as manifestations of a kind of modern 'noble savagery' compatible with twentieth-century styles of life, and could be held up as models for emulation.

At stake here may be a larger issue, with broader cultural resonances. Vague or tentative connections between 'primitivism' and matters mechanical were fairly generally felt in the avant-garde culture of Europe in the early twenties, especially in Paris, and even more especially in attitudes to jazz music. Jazz clearly interested everybody, including Le

Corbusier; and while it may not be literally true that Josephine Baker meant as much to him as grain elevators, she may have meant something similar. Jazz, it would seem, could be regarded as primitively African, in spite of the fact that it came to Paris from North America, but its rhythms – loud, persistent to the point of monotony, and *ostinato* – agreed pretty well with what many avant-garde artists of the time believed to be the rhythms of machinery.

A suggestively complex case in point, from circles close to Le Corbusier, would be the ballet *La Création du monde*, with jazz-inspired music by Darius Milhaud and scenery by Fernand Léger. The latter, while patently and even eruditely inspired by the African art he had sketched in museums, expressed, according to Léger himself, the idea that man is a mechanism like everything else. Beyond that, many of the forms and colours he used in this primitive/mechanical setting seem very close kin to the forms and colours he is known to have admired in mass-produced entertainment art, modern advertising, and automobiles and aircraft. These connections were obviously based on fashion and sentiment, not learning or logic, but by their very ambiguities they provided a rich mixture – out of which the idea of engineering as a form of modern noble savagery could grow – whose homeland, like that of savage/mechanical jazz, could be identified as North America.

These ambiguities, and a general lack of systematic knowledge of the materials under review, freed aesthetes and architects to pick and choose the objects they felt to be truly primitive or properly mechanistic and thus to reject some types of perfectly valid structural procedures, for instance, as corruptions of what they felt to be the true forms of unspoiled engineering. Fundamental aesthetic preferences could still override even the supposedly unquestionable authority that came with the 'objectivity' of engineering design.

So not all works of engineering were indiscriminately admired: the rectangular grids of American factories and the closed cylinders of grain elevators were acceptable, but other types of engineering structures did not suit all modern tastes. The diagonal lattices and tapering trusses of bridges and cranes were unacceptable in some modern Parisian quarters. 'The work of the engineer, pure in its origins, begins gradually to be adulterated by aesthetic pursuits. The crane which

Corn silo, South America.

is seen on this page is soaked in romantic expressionism,' averred an anonymous caption writer in *Cahiers d'Art* in 1926 under an illustration of a spidery but otherwise ordinary German coaling gantry.[18] The comment is the more remarkable since it is perfectly obvious to us now, and must have been equally so then to thoughtful observers, that neither the designers nor the investors in such an installation would be likely to deviate from the strict and objective rationality of economical construction – or profit, if you prefer.

The selective attitude toward the authority of rational industrial structures has an inverted corollary in the architects' attitudes toward one of the most notorious of all topics in the discussion of their architecture, the flat roof. One could reasonably propose that the flat roof became one of the consciously selected symbols of their modernity; and at the highest levels of architectural discourse, the question of flat versus pitched roofs is purely – but explosively – an aesthetic or cultural matter. At a more mundane level, however, such discourse is prone to descend to the simple asseveration that 'everybody knows that flat roofs leak!'

If, as now seems likely and will be argued here, the preferred flat-roofed silhouettes of the International Style derived to some significant degree from the fact that the American industrial buildings they knew from pictures had flat roofs more often than not, then an interesting question is deflected back to the builders of those American factories and warehouses: How could they be so suicidally perverse as to prefer a roof form that contradicted the norms of rationality, economy, and profitability by leaking? And why did the European modernists copy a feature that was, apparently, so unfunctional? Why, in rejecting the splayed lattice legs of the coaling gantry, did they spurn a functional and economical form of construction, while accepting, in the flat roof, a form that was neither?

The answer is that while European flat roofs may indeed have leaked as often as was claimed, the American industrial ones generally did not, and some that I have examined still do not, eighty or more years after their construction. A properly detailed and constructed flat roof can be as stanch as any pitched roof. The actual failure rate of flat roofs in Europe is debatable, and has been much debated.[19] Success in building them, even in rainier northern European climates, dates to several decades before 1900 and thus well before the onset of modernism. If the modernist versions leaked, they must have had some source outside local, current, and commonsense building practices.

This was indeed the case; too many of them were purely formalistic imitations of structures that had never been studied firsthand. Their designers had not seen the originals and had no opportunity to examine and understand how they should be designed, detailed, and constructed. And this brings up a matter of extraordinary historical importance that goes well beyond any scandals about leaking roofs: insofar as the International Style was copied from American industrial prototypes and models, it must be the first architectural movement in the history of the art based almost exclusively on photographic evidence rather than on the ancient and previously unavoidable techniques of personal inspection and measured drawing.

It could, however, be argued that this was entirely appropriate because the power of the photographs comes from the fact that, like the works of engineering they represented, they were understood to be the product of the scientific application of natural laws. Having come into the hands of their European admirers in the guise of news photographs, rather than that of 'art' photography, they were supposedly free from those elements of personal selection and interpretation that must inevitably infect any artistic rendering, or even the traditional production by architectural draftsmen of finished drawings from measured field notes. The photographs represented a truth as apparently objective and modern as that of the functional structures they portrayed.

That, obviously, would be one source of their strength in the eyes of a generation that sought certainty in architecture; but such power to convince usually derives from two other factors: the nature of the objects represented and the expectations of those that look upon those representations. The young radicals of modern Europe clearly believed that they saw here the work of minds as radical as their own; but was this indeed the case? The main burden of this study will be to examine the buildings in question in a way that was not available to Gropius in 1913: firsthand and – as was my good

US Printing Company, Cincinnati.

Grain silo, Bunge y Born, Buenos Aires.

fortune – on the basis of daily familiarity, and with access to the history of the developments that had given them the forms they presented to European eyes. For the American buildings were hardly radical or innovative in the ways that were often supposed; and on closer study the factories, at least, can be seen as the end products of a building tradition whose sources were firmly struck in Europe itself and reached back as far as the later Middle Ages, to the great warehouses of the Hanseatic ports and other multi-storey structures for trade and, later, manufacturing industry. And these great factories were the very end of that tradition, a doomed building type, which, by the time it was taken up in Europe and before Mendelsohn set foot in Buffalo or Detroit, had already ceased to be modern enough to satisfy the needs of innovative American industry.

They were, however, buildings of great quality and power. They were as good as their European admirers had supposed, and one must wonder by what process of photographic divination they managed to recognise these qualities in buildings they had never seen. It is not enough to say that some aspects of these industrial structures chimed in with their aesthetic or stylistic preferences, though it is startling to see how truthful and powerful were, say, Mendelsohn's early and impressionistic sketches of these buildings he had never seen. Aesthetic predisposition may be enough to account for their immediate impact on that generation, but it is not enough when one stands in front of the buildings themselves. They do have an almost Egyptian monumentality in many cases, and in abandonment and death they evoke the majesties of a departed civilisation. Or so it used to seem to me, looking downstream on the Buffalo River from the angle of South Street. On either side of the water, like an avenue of mighty tombs, were structures representing almost the whole history of the grain elevator; certainly, no other city in the world possessed so concentrated a set of historically valuable elevators as Buffalo then did, along that half mile of river down to the Ohio Street Bridge. It was a privilege to know them in their ravaged antique grandeur, just as it was to work in Buffalo, for however short a period, in a classic and sophisticated example of a 'Daylight' factory. Whatever the shortcomings of its antique heating system and ill-used windows that blew open during blizzards and filled my office with snow, the factory's columned interior had a grave pre-Classical regularity that did indeed look as if it might contain some ancient secret law of great architecture.

I was moved by these buildings, and that was partly because I came upon them unprepared. They were as unknown to me as they must be to any student or lover of architecture because, outside the modernists' polemics of the twenties, they have practically no part in the records of architectural history and have yet to draw a critic worthy of their austere virtues. That is regrettable, for they deserve a better fate than to be left to the industrial archaeologists and prettifying rehabilitators who seem at present to be the only parties with any interest in them. They need to be brought back among 'the canons of giant architecture', and they deserve far more respect and honour than they commonly receive in America, for – as much as the work of a Richardson or a Wright – they represent the triumph of what is American in American building art.

Grain elevators, sketches by Erich Mendelsoh, 1914–15.

They also represent one of the earliest and most powerful influences of American building art on the rest of the world. The impact of HH Richardson or Frank Lloyd Wright, for instance, has been extensively studied and documented because they were acknowledged to be great architects and were expected to affect the work of other creative talents. The factories and grain elevators, however, seem to have been influential precisely because they were thought to derive from some subculture that did not normally connect to the high culture of architects and other artists. And, insofar as these supposedly nonarchitectural industrial buildings may have helped to fix the forms and usages of what we now call 'The International Style', which has so far been the dominant style of twentieth-century architecture, Americans owe them the same degree of respect they award other native arts that have affected the rest of the world, such as the Hollywood film, dance theatre, and jazz.

Ultimately, however, our study must return to the European modernists themselves. They were the ones who made the International Style international and finally brought it back to North America in the thirties. Furthermore, it was they who had set up the categories and attitudes with which I – a well-trained child of their modern movement but an uninformed stranger – came to the Concrete Atlantis and was moved by its monuments. Any search for an understanding of why those factories and elevators look so good to us now must also involve some attempt to understand the ambitions, expectations, and frame of mind that drove the founding fathers of the modern movement to adopt these monuments as the models for their new architecture – which was also, somehow, expected to rediscover and then embody the eternal and fundamental verities underlying all great architecture, old as well as new.

No more striking testimony of this paradoxical mind-set can be found than the text with which this book concludes: Edoardo Persico's encomium on the Fiat factory in Turin. Familiar with its interior operations as a daily employee but apparently unaware that it was designed in deliberate imitation of an American factory (since he never mentions the fact), he nevertheless finds in it intimations of order, even a divine order like that of the Gothic cathedrals. In this building that was to become a *locus classicus* of modernism and a place of pilgrimage for modernists, who liked to have themselves photographed on its rooftop racetrack as proof that they were indeed *moderner Menschen*, Persico found, among its concrete columns and under the stare of its enormous windows, compelling evidence of 'an ancient order of... obedience to the Laws.'

Continental Motor Manufacturing Company, Detroit, Michigan.

Elevators on the Buffalo River; view downstream from South Street.

1   John Steinbeck, *Cannery Row* (Penguin, 1973), pp 143–4.
2   The structure has now been removed and the site cleared to accommodate road realignments in connection with the new Monterey Aquarium.
3   Richard Etlin, 'Le Corbusier, Choisy and the Architectural Promenade', paper delivered at the annual conference of the Society of Architectural Historians, Pittsburgh, PA, April 1985.
4   Robert Venturi, Denise Scott-Brown and Steven Izenour, *Learning from Las Vegas* (MIT Press, 1972), pp 92–3.
5   Walter Gropius, 'Die Entwicklung Moderner Industriebaukunst', English translation as 'The Development of Modern Industrial Architecture', in Tim Benton, Charlotte Benton and Dennis Sharp eds, *Form and Function: A Source Book for the History of Architecture and Design 1890–1939* (Crosby Lockwood Staples, 1975), pp 53–4.
6   Le Corbusier, *Towards a New Architecture*, translated by Frederick Etchells (John Rodker, 1927), p 33.
7   Eric Mendelsohn, *Letters of an Architect*, edited by Oskar Beyer (Abelard-Schuman, 1967), p 69.
8   Le Corbusier, p 33.
9   Francis Bacon, 'The New Atlantis', in *Essays and New Atlantis*, edited by Gordon Sherman Haight (Walter J Black, 1942), p 264.
10 Le Corbusier, p 33.
11 Walter Gropius, pp 53-4.
12 See, for instance, the various papers from 'Das Andere' anthologised by Loos himself in *Trotzdem*, 1931, pp 11–50.
13 See 'Die Kunst in Industrie und Handel', the *Jahrbuch des Deutschen Werkbundes* (Eugen Diederichs, 1913); the insert of illustrations follows p 16.
14 Letter in the archive of Le Corbusier, Paris, reported to me by Jacques Paul and Joyce Lowman.
15 Walter Curt Behrendt, *Der Sieg des Neuen Baustils* (Dr Fr Wedekind & Co, 1927), p 22.
16 Vincent Scully, *American Architecture and Urbanism* (Thames and Hudson, 1969), p 123. This illustration and its caption neatly encapsulate the passage of these images into the mythology of modern architecture and their absorption into American architectural culture. Scully, needing only to make a general point about American grain elevators, which he could have illustrated by sending out a student with a camera, nevertheless uses one of the Gropius images, as altered by Le Corbusier, and then captions it as being in Buffalo, whereas it still stood, at that time, in Montreal!
17 Le Corbusier, p 33.
18 *Cahiers d'Art* 5, 1926, p 114.
19 For a judicious account of the German debates on the flat roof, see Richard Pommer, 'The Flat Roof', in *Art Journal* 43, no 2, Summer 1983, pp 155–69.

Alice Twemlow
Banham's Pedagogy on the Page

//

Reyner Banham
O, Bright Star...

Published in *New Society*, 5 May 1983, pp 188–9.

Alice Twemlow
Banham's Pedagogy on the Page

Reyner Banham did much of his teaching in the pages of *New Society*, *New Statesman* and *The Architectural Review*. His unsmirking scrutiny of the British potato crisp, Californian surfboards, paperback book covers, commercial signage and the decoration of ice cream trucks, shared in engagingly vivid language in general interest publications throughout the 1960s and 70s, democratised critical writing about art, architecture and design.

The thing about teaching on the page is that it can continue and even flourish more completely long after its intended sell-by-date. Ensuing generations of design historians have benefitted from Banham's rearrangement and expansion of the canon. In my own case, it was in the mid-1990s and via my own tutors, Penny Sparke and Gillian Naylor, at the Royal College of Art and the Victoria and Albert Museum in London. The realisation that the 'noisy ephemeridae' of everyday life could be my subject matter was formative and supported my interests at the time, among them the production and circulation of 1990s club flyers or 1960s TV title sequences.[1]

But perhaps even more important than this extension of the 'long front of culture'[2], with a focus on 'goodies' instead of 'good design',[3] was what he did in the way he wrote. Through extolling the virtues of the exposed engine components of a Buick V8 engine, for example, he also lifted the hood on his own writerly toolset. He laid bare the mechanics of his critical and empirical research process as a way to empower a reader to better understand and engage in the critique of architecture and design, or to 'carry [the] discipline down from Olympus into the market-place', as he once put it.[4] Whether you were a student, an architect or a gas engineer, you could read along and learn how to identify a research question based on a hunch, track down an elusive detail to its source, wield vocabulary to one's purpose – whether it existed yet or not. You were encouraged to see and evaluate your own designed environment – from the mega to the micro – in all its problematic or joyful, but always fascinating and complex, reality.

In 'O Bright Star...', a 1983 *New Society* essay about the design of a sheriff's badge, he describes his research journey step by step, from the moment the decoration of the badge excites his curiosity and he identifies 'the problem of who designs sheriffs' stars', to the explanation of his dogged pursuit of the wellspring of its design and manufacturing via libraries, police authorities, a factory's pattern shop. This adventure finally leads to his realisation, as the result of an overheard telephone call, that the badge was, in effect, designed by the Acme Star and Badge Co secretary.

The generosity conveyed by this kind of disclosure of expertise blurs the distinction between writer and reader, historian and critic, architect and citizen, and teacher and student. That, to my mind, is the 'bright star' by which pedagogy should be guided.

1   Reyner Banham, 'Vehicles of Desire', in *Art*, 1 September 1955, p 3.
2   From an essay by Lawrence Alloway, 'The Long Front of Culture', in *Cambridge Opinion*, no 17, 1959, pp 25–6, in which he argued that the carefully guarded separations between high and low culture, 'frozen in layers in a pyramid', had been melted into the 'continuum' of mass media.
3   Reyner Banham, 'Who is this "Pop"?', in *Motif*, Winter 1962–63, p 13.
4   Reyner Banham, 'Foreword', in *Design by Choice: Ideas in Architecture*, edited by Penny Sparke (Academy Editions, 1981), p 7.

REYNER BANHAM
O, BRIGHT STAR...

...of constabular authority, resplendent on the uniformed bosom of the female deputy sheriff who had just meticulously hand-checked my carry-on luggage. *Hand*-checked – no x-rays or metal detectors; they keep up the ancient skills and value-systems in that high inter-mountain country where Marlboro Men roam in their pick-up trucks and elegantly-worn blue denim. Indeed, it's all so macho and hairy-chested that you have to wonder how they ever managed to deputise a *woman*...

Musing on these matters while waiting for Sagebrush Airways flight 665 to whisk us away to less arid climes, I watched her go back into her office and close the brown plywood door behind her. On the door was a very much enlarged version of the same star of authority, about 18 inches across, presumably a plastic decal to go on the side of a patrol car.

This badge of authority bore looking at: like all good sheriff stars it had points, six of them. The points had round knobs on their extremities, and the triangular spaces within them were filled in with distinctly Victorian foliate decoration. And there were words, like *Sheriff* and *Robson County*, on scrolls, surrounding the Great Seal of the State in the centre.

It is not often that one has a chance to study such an object in magnified detail like this – to get an equally good look at the one the deputy was wearing I would have had to lean close enough to get myself arrested.

Neat, I thought; fascinating. But the pleasure of seeing a sheriff star under a microscope, as it were, was suddenly terminated by a dread thought which persistently afflicts all those who profess the trade of design-historian: *Who designed it?* Sheriff stars can't just happen; some person or group had made decisions, based on taste or tradition, standing orders or divine revelation, and had thus determined its form and iconography.

And I had no idea who. Similar horrors of ignorance have doubtless afflicted persons of my calling confronted with the brightwork on British bobbies' bonce-cosies, or the heraldry on the reverse of Maria Theresa dollars, or all that squiggly stuff around Her Britannic Majesty's Principal Secretary of State inside the front cover of your passport, but I was stuck, there and then, with the problem of who designs sheriff stars.

It's taken a long time to find out, because a certain reticence surrounds the whole topic. There is no literature that I or our indefatigable campus library staff have been able to turn up, and bare-faced inquiries directed at law enforcement personnel tend to get very dusty answers – don't ask a policeman, because he will immediately suspect the worst; there are far too many unlicensed stars and badges in circulation already.

In the end, it was the sheriff of Salinas, caught with his guard down when my credentials were up, who broke the silence and told me where his department went to buy their insignia, and this lead (the appropriate cliche, you'll agree) led me to Acme Star and Badge Co, and that's not their real name either, but the company's reticence is catching.

Actually it led me in the first place to a telephone conversation with the company secretary, who sent me their catalogue, which confirmed that I had indeed got on to the right kind of operation, and then to an extended conversation with the proprietor, which confirmed that I had also got on to an enthusiast – to put it very mildly indeed.

I probably should have guessed this last from the rhetoric in the trade-literature I had already received:

'All of our badges are hand-made and use silver solder for ribbons, attachments etc, and these consume enormous amounts of silver. Since our solders are 45 per cent and 66 per cent silver these costs reflect ultimately in the price.

We could change our methods of construction and utilise lead solder but that would just make an inferior product, and in this plastic world quality will not be eliminated at Acme Star and Badge Co. The only companies that remain in business are firms that are serious about their craftsmanship.'

In this plastic world, it turns out, about a dozen companies in the whole of North America are serious enough about their craftsmanship to have survived, four of them here in California, and mostly firms about the same size as Acme, with an output of less than 10,000 pieces a year. Not quite a cottage industry, then; more like the little maisters in Sheffield, only in this case spread across a continent.

Not that the premises were anything like Sheffield, when I got to them: three 1920ish single-storey shop units on an island of older development amid all the urban renewal in downtown Oakland. The firm was founded before the turn of the century, but has only been on this site since 1971, when it was urban-renewed out of its old building, and the present proprietor has only been in charge since 1968. The entirely convincing air of unshakable traditionalism that pervades the operation may thus be no more than an optical illusion by now (the old shops must have been comfortably wellworn before they moved in) or it may be generated by the process of manufacture, as we shall see.

The first impression on entering the front office is that you have walked into a badge freak's paradise. In the glass display case on the wall are some 100 badges and stars, some labelled as being from the early 1900s, while under the glazed top of the counter opposite are another 120 or more, loose on jewellers' trays. Pay-dirt for the badge design-historian, but how to mine and refine it?

A TIMELESS WORLD

The more you look at this board the less sense of orderly stylistic or technical development you can discern. Some of the most ornately Victorian are clearly recent, some of the most obviously modern-movement, in plain undecorated silver with stern sanserif lettering, are among the oldest on display.

Perhaps we are looking at a world of design that has become timeless, frozen out of the tides of fashion. But if that is so, then whence the very large variety of different designs, not at all the narrow range that would normally come from a static vernacular?

The answer, again, lies in the production process, which is in itself something of an historical monument. The raw stock is bronze strip, plated with the appropriate gold, silver or alloy on one face, and the blank star is punched out on it on a Roussell punch – which, like most of the machinery employed, comes from Providence, Rhode Island, another bit of American traditionalism. The blank is then taken to a Standard Machines die-press, and the foliated decoration in the points is bashed into relief on it. Three or four thumps are needed to make the embossing deep enough, and since the metal work hardens, it has to be taken away and annealed between thumps, acquiring a coating of oxide that dulls it to anything but a bright star.

Then another thumping press raises its centre into a dome, if that is what's required. The lettering is drawn on by hand, meticulously with a sharp-pointed scriber, to ensure its just spacing and proper arrangement before it is punched into the metal with hand-held letter-punches, a small hammer and finicky precision. This done, the recessed letter-forms are filled-in a positively mediaeval way – with a slurry of coloured ground glass and water, and popped into a minute and non-mediaeval electric oven in order to fire the slurry into enamel.

The now more-or-less complete badge or star comes out of the oven looking like an archaeological relic, all blackened and blotchy. But some smart fettling by hand, before it goes into a tumbler to be sloshed around with a quart or two of steel balls to take out every minutest scratch or blemish, and out comes as supernaturally gleaming a star of authority as you could ever hope to see.

Now, this technology permits someone to do quite a lot of designing without ever having to put pencil to paper. Where dies, ribbons, etc, are compatible, a good deal of mix and match is possible – decorative devices can be selected, rejected, omitted, for instance, or the same infill patterns can be applied to stars with or without knobs on their points, the whole thing could be domed or flat, and so on. The possible variations are, theoretically, a mathematical product of the numbers of compatible dies, and there are supposed to be at least 300 assorted dies on the shelves along the workshop wall (it looked a lot more to me) and there are thought to be about the same number in the 'archive' or 'mausoleum' of abandoned patterns.

Currently, Acme are recovering old designs from the archive and finding them saleable, which is one reason for the historical confusions. Another is the fact that rather few absolutely new designs are being created from scratch because they have lost their old die-cutter, and failed to find anyone trained to work at his bench, in spite of advertising as far afield as Germany. They can farm out their die-cutting, but I got a distinct impression that they don't really care to do that; it would be a concession to the plastic world, somehow.

Whether the cutting of totally innovative designs was ever common I now take leave to doubt, and at the moment it is patently unnecessary. For the foreseeable future, Acme should be able to cruise along on its large visible stock of existing designs and variations, and the hidden assets of the mausoleum – especially in the present conservative (not to say nostalgic) climate of opinion out in Law'n'Order-land. That still leaves the design-historian with his ultimate problem, however: accepting that day-to-day designing is done by choosing motifs from catalogue and archive, where did those motifs come from in the first place?

DEPUTY SHERIFF
TULARE COUNTY
200

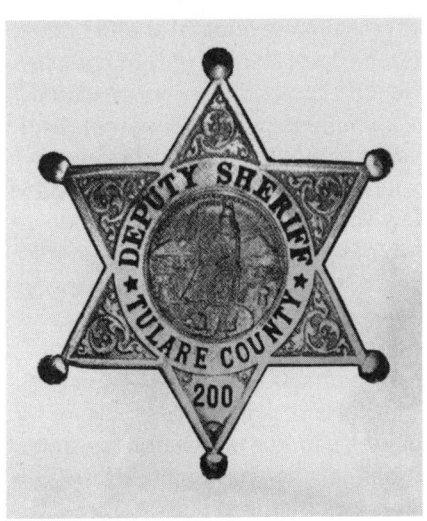

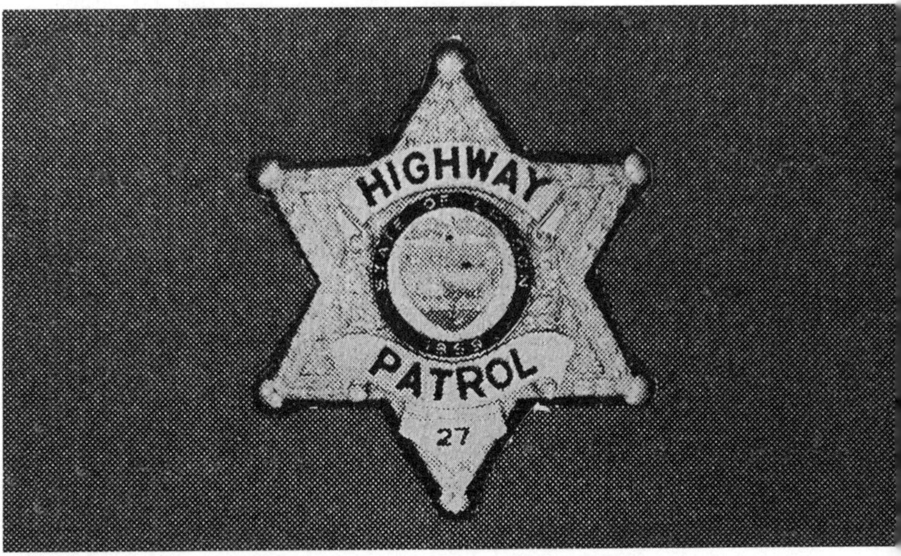
HIGHWAY
PATROL
27

Are they all variations from some unique original sheriff badge, some kind of *Ur-stern* or Platonic Idea shining untarnished in the dawn's early light of American law-enforcement? It would be tempting to think of it as something profoundly simple and unadorned, but that temptation should be resisted because – as far as I can ascertain – such a badge would have been made in the early 1850s (when New York police are first described as wearing stars) and would therefore be likely to be crusted with early Victorian ornament, acanthus leaves flourishing in every point, plaited borders on every edge, droopy scrolls for the lettering – something like Acme's present No. 646 as worn by the Oregon Highway Patrol, perhaps.

I doubt we will ever know; the origins of this prized emblem are probably lost behind a jungle of foliation, borders, state seals, scrolls, ribbons, heraldic beasts, sunbursts, republican eagles ... and bitter arguments about whether to have five, six or seven points. Those arguments are still proceeding, or something very like them – while I was perusing Acme's stock of stars and badges, the company secretary was on the phone, burning the ears off someone at a local YMCA about the arrangement of the lettering on their official seal:

'No way; the "Founded 1897" should go around the bottom of the circle, right? Then the "YMCA" goes across the middle, and "Commerceville" goes around the top, OK? Oh, you're welcome, but you shoulda asked me first 'cause I could have told you all that stuff.'

I think I heard an official seal being designed. If I'd hung around a bit longer, perhaps I might have heard a sheriff star being designed? Within a settled idiom, design does not necessarily require drawings, but that's something they dare not tell you at the Royal College of Art or its American equivalents. It's only originality that needs drawings!

Kersten Geers
Giving and Taking

//

Reyner Banham
Revelation

Published in *Scenes in America Deserta*, 1982, p 68.

Kersten Geers
Giving and Taking

Reyner Banham gave me America.

    When Ábalos and Herreros introduced me to Banham as a student, it was the cover of the book *Los Angeles: The Architecture of Four Ecologies* that caught all my attention. The book and its ideas were presented as part of a lecture series at the ETSAM in Madrid, together with a family of other authors and books and ideas in search of some sort of theory-in-the making about architecture. Or so it seemed. Most of this theory found its way into *The Good Life*, written by Iñaki Ábalos. I tend to think this book was published 'posthumously' to Ábalos' collaboration with Herreros, but in reality it was published earlier, though still quite some years after my time as a student. At the ETSAM, *Los Angeles: The Architecture of Four Ecologies* was presented as a window into the US, Banham as our guide. I did not understand much, my Spanish was not good enough. The cover of the book, showing *A Bigger Splash* by David Hockney, was mesmerising. A mysterious yet convincing composition of hedonistic life without figures, scorching heat depicted in basic colour hues, a picture of the city via the pool.

    The next year I went to the US and only visited Los Angeles and the desert. Hockney's painting, removed from the book in subsequent reprints, anticipates Banham's 'pictorial' gaze. Hockney's works in the 1950s and 60s are so composed, so curated, framed, that they succeed in some form of basic storytelling. They 'show' what is not told. They talk about people and relations and culture through simple depictions of things (and some figures); the still picture as a door to the world. It made a perfect introduction to Banham's writing. The fragmented, composed view of different ecologies is a case in point. In all of his writings there is a strange and radical juxtaposition of things and landscapes, buildings and people; everything is equal, everything is equally important, as if in some grandiose balancing act. Everything matters, nothing matters, everything is the same: the city, the landscape, people, architecture are all part of some gigantic experiment in cohabitation, but one that has mostly dark sides.

Scenes in America Deserta is a book hidden in plain sight. Published in the wake of Banham's success, outside the canon of his books of architectural theory and history, the book felt like a postscript, revisiting for a last time all the big ideas about land and landscape, taking stock of the powers of each. Banham has always discovered the world through his own constructions and compositions. Driven by the fiction of ideas, the book gives a glimpse into the backstage of things. The world without projections, the world we should care about, today perhaps more urgently than when, in the swinging 1960s, ecologies were merely an opportunity. The 'revelation' quoted here tells us everything at once. An imaginary figure of a rock photographed reveals a technical box, unseen when the picture was taken. Architecture and the world forever intertwined, but also in some sense only there when we want to see it, as a perpetual *Fata Morgana*.

REYNER BANHAM
REVELATION

On one of the slides from our first visit to Four Corners country, there is a building. That was not why we took that shot; the intention was to photograph 'Phone Booth Mesa' (more properly 'Chimney Rock', but every fifth outcrop in the Southwest seems to be called that!) on the way up from Shiprock to Cortez. Neither of us remembers seeing any building in the foreground of that view; but there it is: one standard, off-the-peg, industrially-produced Butler building with an air conditioner unit on its flatly-pitched roof. It is finished in an inoffensive tan colour, but that doesn't make it any less outstandingly visible against the background of sagebrush. Why then does the eye of memory not see it? It must be that it is such a usual building in a landscape where only the exotic or the outrageous in architecture tends to look at home and be remembered.

Albert Narath
Solar Futures Past: Banham on Baer

//

Reyner Banham
The Sage of Corrales

Published in *New Society*, 17 March 1983, pp 430–1.

Albert Narath
Solar Futures Past: Banham on Baer

Up a dirt road, there are horse paddocks, stacks of cordwood and piles of adobe. Abandoned equipment is scattered, rusted out, across the arid brush. And then there is the house itself, a glittering geodesic crust set on a bluff above the village of Corrales, New Mexico, along the Rio Grande on the outskirts of the city of Albuquerque. This is the setting for Reyner Banham's visit to Steve and Holly Baer's Zome House in winter 1982, published the following year in one of his numerous short contributions to the magazine *New Society*.

The article is not well known today, hidden in the far nooks and crannies of the expansive Banham bibliography. There are good reasons, however, to revisit Banham's interpretation of the Baer house. For one, it allows us to consider the place of solar energy within Banham's career-long preoccupation with the subject of modern architecture and technology. This is more than a purely historiographic exercise. In recent years, architects, curators and historians have frequently positioned the upsurge of interest in energy-conscious and ecological approaches to design in the US during the late-1960s and 70s as a convenient point of departure for genealogies of 'sustainable', 'ecological' or 'green' design. The Baer house in particular, no doubt due in part to its memorable geometrical form and its connection to the countercultural movements of the era, has drawn increased historical interest. At the time of this writing, the Baers continue to live in the house and consider it an ongoing experiment rather than a finished work. Nevertheless, it is most often cast as an architectural artefact – a monument to solar futures past.

After its initial construction in 1972, the Baer house quickly emerged as an icon of the solar design and appropriate technology movements that flourished in the southwestern part of the United States around the oil crises of the 1970s. Images of the building's distinctive south-facing façade circulated internationally in popular design magazines, solar energy publications, various countercultural and owner-builder venues, and in Steve Baer's own book *Sunspots*. A decade later, Banham himself snapped a picture of the house from the same vantage point during his visit. In the photograph, the house is indistinguishable from its passive solar technologies. Water-filled barrel 'drumwalls', flip-down aluminium-faced shutters, louvres and various solar collectors scattered around the site do their thing, quietly soaking up and storing the energy of winter light. The building has the countenance of a gizmo, recalling Banham's description in the 1965 essay 'The Great Gizmo' of a 'small self-contained unit of high performance in relation to its size and cost, whose function is to transform some undifferentiated set of circumstances to a condition nearer human desires.'[1]

It is tempting to connect the Baer house to the other design objects – from the Franklin Stove, to the cordless shaver, to the Toyota Land Cruiser and Clark Cortez camper – which comprise Banham's sweeping genealogy of North American technology and settlement in that well-known essay. The Baer house, however, resists any such neat contextualisation. Its eclectic, hand-built surfaces contrast with the smooth lines and clean packages characteristic of American industrial design. And unlike the other objects in 'The Great Gizmo', it would never be embraced within mainstream culture. If the bold formal language of the Baer House was initially publicised as the embodiment of an architectural future where American design ingenuity would reach its fruition through the harnessing of local energy sources in opposition to the extraction, distribution and consumption of fossil fuels, then by the time Banham visited the building, it had become emblematic of a future that would not be fulfilled. With ebbing public interest in energy-conscious design and the termination of federally funded solar research programmes after the inauguration of Ronald Reagan in 1980, experiments like the Baer house became increasingly isolated. When Banham took in the sweeping view of Albuquerque from the site, the city was already decisively shaped by the dispersed planning model of the strip mall and the single-family suburban house, all fed by an expanding electrical grid. Directly across from the Baers' property, Banham would have also seen the rapidly growing chip fabrication plant developed by the Intel Corporation, which had been lured to the area in 1980 through the promise of cheap land, tax incentives and abundant low-cost energy.

For Banham, the Baer house was no less than the 'founding monument' of the American solar energy movement, but it also posed a distinct interpretive challenge.[2] The publication of the *New Society* piece marks a period of transition in his writing. Published a year after the book *Scenes in America Deserta*, the article can be seen in the context of Banham's personal infatuation with the landscapes and design cultures of the American desert.[3] It also coincided with his preparation of the second edition of the book *The Architecture of the Well-tempered Environment*, which included a significant new section on solar design and the energy crisis centred on a consideration of the Baer house. There, the project represents a direct rebuttal to the energy intensiveness of then-recent developments such as the high tech movement and the popularity of inflatable structures. From a historical perspective,

Banham argued that the Baer house benefitted from a connection to a technology that 'goes back in the US at least as far as the pre-Columbian Indians'.[4] The deep legacy of solar design that he traced in New Mexico was difficult to reconcile, however, with existing genealogies of architectural modernism. It is noteworthy, in this respect, that instead of illustrating the Baer house with the picture he took during his visit, Banham intentionally chose a view taken by the architect Jeffrey Cook before shingle cladding was added to the building's aluminum panels. This encouraged an easier visual association with the monuments of the early 20th century, and especially the crystalline expressionism of Paul Sheerbart and Bruno Taut. But the resonances only go so far – the Baer house clearly confounded many of the received categories associated with the reception of architectural modernism by architects and historians. To name only a few, it confused distinctions between high-tech and low-tech, extraction and consumption, and the professional domains of architectural design and environmental control engineering. In his contribution to *New Society*, these interpretive difficulties are extended to Steve Baer himself, whose approach to technology, mystique within the solar scene and personal politics similarly resisted any kind of neat historical packaging. Reflecting on his visit, Banham finds meaning in the discordant experience of being served dinner at 'a decent antique table... with decent flatware, decent stemware, napery and candle' while sitting in an experimental aluminium-clad hexagonal dome that had been widely celebrated as the harbinger of a new radical solar avant-garde.[5]

    We might see in Banham's grappling with the meaning and legacy of the Baer house a more far-reaching attempt to come to terms with the place of energy-conscious design, as well as the legacy of 1970s appropriate technology experimentation, in architectural history. In thinking about the significance of the project and its reception in the decade since it was built, Banham was forced to confront not only the genealogies of architectural modernism that he had worked to construct since the publication of *Theory and Design in the First Machine Age* in 1960, but also some of the basic methodologies that had informed his interpretations as an architectural historian.[6] The eco-political context of Banham's engagement with Baer in the wake of the energy crises of the 1970s is different in important ways than the conditions surrounding the environmental challenges we face today. At the same time, as historians increasingly call for the creation of new methodologies in light of outsized human-caused impacts to the environment, Banham's experience at the Baer house has the potential to be instructive.

1   Reyner Banham, 'The Great Gizmo', in *Industrial Design*, September 1965, pp 48–59.
2   Reyner Banham, *The Architecture of the Well-tempered Environment*, 2nd edition (University of Chicago Press, 1984), p 284.
3   Reyner Banham, *Scenes in America Deserta* (Gibbs M Smith and Thames and Hudson, 1982).
4   Reyner Banham, *The Architecture of the Well-tempered Environment*, p 278.
5   Reyner Banham, 'The Sage of Corrales', in *New Society*, 17 March 1983, p 431.
6   Reyner Banham, *Theory and Design in the First Machine Age* (The Architectural Press, 1960).

REYNER BANHAM
THE SAGE OF CORRALES

Much of New Mexico is laid out in the same tidy rectangles as the rest of the United States, but the township of Corrales, for ancestral reasons, is parcelled out in long narrow strips running back from the banks of the Rio Grande. Each strip has been developed separately from its neighbours – there must be 20 or more houses on some of them – and their sandy service roads, running back through scrappy orchards and horse-paddocks, past solid adobes and woodsy bungalows, are the streets of Corrales.

Most peter out finally in confusion and wrecked autos, but one or two actually make it back to the crest of the modest bluff that frames the broad valley on that side, and from the top you can see huge views over the valley, the ancient Indian pueblos, the wide shallow river sparkling in the arid sunshine and, like a mighty backdrop, the wrinkled flank of the Sandia mountain on the farther side. Up at this commanding level are the newest houses in the town, but they look edgily to the south, not towards the mountain, because this is the sacred heartland of the solar housing movement.

Most are pretty routine examples (whatever their owners/builders/designers may claim) of the solar genre, with large areas of sloping glass to the south, boring backsides to the north, and abandoned lumps of equipment cluttering the surrounding desert. Except for the one at our feet right now. Even the litter on the site is different – that old school bus, for instance, with the remains of a smarty-pants geometrical paint-job, is one of the great movement-buses of the late sixties and early seventies.

No, *not* Ken Kesey. This is Steve Baer's house, 'the first major architectural manifestation of the newly-found solar ethic... of 1972.' Around the house itself is a classic desert garden, terraced out of the brow of the bluff, tan and grey with neatly raked sand between the spare but elegant cacti and bushes, and the house itself is something else – a cluster of eleven roughly hexagonal domes covered in wooden shingles and garnished at seeming random with curved, sail-like reflectors over skylights.

Since the house sits low on the terrace under the crest, the effect of all this from up here is distinctly troglodytic and weird; something tile-hung is bubbling up out of the ground with a flourish of high technology on its crust. Appearance doesn't altogether deceive, either; this 'Zome-House' was – and still is – headed in some very different directions from all other solar houses, just as Baer himself is at variance with the tribe of would-be followers who tried to make him the cult-leader of The Solar Thing.

That historic bus is a relic of the days when *Zome!* was the rallying cry for an attempt to put a simplified version of Buckminster Fuller's subtle and mathematically difficult domes within the reach of everyman. With the pragmatism that has marked all his work, Baer threw out the subtlety with the maths, and came up with a coarse-cut dome whose geometries were within the intellectual grasp of sharp high-school drop-outs, buildable by *homo habilis* without a long apprenticeship.

By the time this L-shaped Zome-cluster was built, however, Baer had gone on from Construction to Energy. The Zomes were built on a massive heat-storing concrete slab, and were lined up to shoulder height with heat-storing adobe walls, except where they were hugely glazed on the sunward side. Not for the view, but to grab the sun's heat, which is stored in dozens of 55-gallon oil drums full of water, stacked in giant wine-racks just inside the glass. Outside the glass are well-sized fold-down shutters of polished aluminium, to reflect more sun-heat on the water-wall as they lie flat by day, and to lock that heat in when they are raised at night.

GIZMOLOGIES AND SNUGGLE-UPS

In the ensuing ten years the house has gained more insulation everywhere (hence the shingles on the formerly shiny domes) and all kinds of smart technologies to collect and control more heat (hence the reflecting sails on the roof) because it can get very cold indeed at these altitudes. But as a result of all these gizmologies and snuggle-ups, Baer has cut his fuel consumption from about a cord a year to less than a quarter-cord.

A quarter-*what*? Those who know their American traditions will know that a cord of firewood is a stack of split logs four feet by eight feet by four feet, loose-packed enough for a mouse to run through, but 'not so darn loose the cat can git after him!' To find this bucolic unit for measure, redolent of rustic crafts (and rural honesty!), cropping up in the middle of a conversation about the state of the art in energy management may sound a bit like 'talking bushels and pecks in outer space', but it's entirely appropriate here. When the Baers need more heat than the house can trap from the sun, they light a wood-burning stove – and that says a lot about the grass roots of the energy movement in the United States, and its present discontents.

Originally, around 1970, the emphasis on supposedly 'low' or 'soft' technologies, like burning wood instead of oil, was part of the general radical-left revolt against conglomerates, multinationals, the military-industrial complex. Anyone who listened carefully, however, would soon begin to sense that the constant emphasis on household or even individual self-sufficiency – 'unplugging from the utilities rip-off' – seemed to be pointing in a different direction from the communitarian and collectivist goals the left normally cherishes.

Uncomfortably recalling the armed paranoids in California with their well-stocked radiation shelters, many of those who took off to avoid big business in desert communes seemed obsessed with survival technologies that would shield them from the imminent (but not necessarily atomic) apocalypse of capitalism to come. At its most rabid, this sounded like pure Darwinian selfishness, but protest makes strange bedfellows, and while everybody was paranoid about the same things ('General Motors, General Electric, General Foods and… er… General Westmoreland!') the movement could hang together.

A decade later, the strains are showing, and the left aren't speaking to Baer any more. A lot of people told me, wonderingly, 'He's like a born-again conservative now!' In a sense they are right – he's in business as a producer and consultant on solar devices, and though he still reads the *American Spectator*, he clearly believes in the virtues of the market and opposes government intervention therein, suspects all kinds of groups and doesn't hesitate to tell you so, and seems to go along with Reagan's policies, albeit warily.

The Baer house, New Mexico, from the collection of Reyner Banham's photographs held in the archive of the Architectural Association.

Such things have happened to many an old-time radical, I thought, as I watched Mrs Baer setting a decent antique table for dinner with decent flatware, decent stem-ware, napery and candles, but I beg leave to doubt he's been born again. The man, I suspect, always was a conservative at heart, and those who don't speak to him now mistook him rather profoundly in the heady days of the Zomeworks bus.

The last previous time I had seen that bus had been at the Aspen Design conference of 1970, a rather twitchy gathering marked by, among other things, the glacial *de-haut-en-bas* contumely with which the French delegation had treated all manifestations of the American eco-movement. Some of their reasons for doing so were impeccable: the movement was not French and it was not Marxist, and that ought to have been conclusive. But they overcooked their case *un peu* by insisting that there was no moral difference between environmentalism and the use of napalm in Vietnam. In their more lucid moments, though, they clearly perceived that, far from being radical, US environmentalism was already individualistic, property-oriented, conservative and defensive. 'Established power,' said their manifesto 'has *always* fought against pollution… of the Establishment itself!'

Wood-burning Baer, if you had no idea of his earlier radical entanglements, could easily be taken for a paragon of those old Protestant and craggy New England virtues of thrift, self-reliance, seriousness and moral certainty that most of us sneakily admire or envy. If I read him aright he is not born again nor in any other way changed; the Sage of Corrales has to his own self been true. If the movement now *needs* traitors (in itself a bad sign) then it might have more bloodthirsty fun baiting Amory ('Soft Energy Paths') Lovins.

And if it hasn't yet identified Lovins as a defector, it's probably because he still uses the language of liberalism. Frankly, myself had not recognised where he was headed since the old Alternative Technology days, until he turned up in one of those fawning *Love-that-Jet-Set* articles that you only find in airline magazines. This was on the way back from the New Mexico trip, so the contrast with Baer was the more piquant, as I read how he and his (how did you guess?) horse-riding lawyer-spouse now serve as consultants to governments and presidents and… utility companies and energy conglomerates, and moved to Aspen (oh, there's an irony!) not only because it has a sushi bar but because its little airport (a solar-heated disaster, by the way) is only 35 air-minutes from Denver International.

And so on, gush after gush, and especially about the 3,800 square feet of solar-heated combined house and think-tank they are building on a couple of acres of land just up the valley from Aspen proper.

Nice work if they can get it, huh? Yes, indeed – but there is no way that anyone who can afford two acres of accessible and serviced land anywhere such a Fat City as Aspen can possibly identify with the poor and downtrodden of the earth. Gone are the days when Hunter Thompson could nearly get elected sheriff by mobilising the Woodland Freak vote; Aspen hasn't been that sort of place for over a decade now, and maybe that wouldn't be the sort of place the Lovinses would like anyhow. But I think there may be loud howls of betrayal if that article should ever fall into the hands of these who don't speak to Baer any more. Certainly, it bothered me, atavistically, in a way my conversations in Corrales did not.

What did bother me at Corrales was that view across the valley – or, rather, the absence of it. As I came down the sandy service road again I just had to stop and admire its size, its sweep, its artfully simple composition, with just enough signs of human habitation down below to emphasise the remote enormity of the long mountain beyond. How could he build a house with so much glass, yet only a couple of small rectangles clear for viewing? Oh sure, he can go out onto his elegantly raked terrace and look at the view, but that seems to me to miss one of the great promises of architecture, which is to be able to enjoy Nature without having to be out in it.

In this, at least it seems to me, Baer is not so much a conservative as a determined modernist; quite as determined as those in the twenties who built in steel, or made long cantilevers, or windows that went round corners, not for the sake of a fairer human habitat, but to prove a polemical point. Those racks of sun-warmed oil-drums make, and over-make, his point about heat storage. They even look quite decorative, but they do prevent you looking at the mountain while you sit at that well-laid table. No doubt this thought has occurred to other visitors, but you won't find it mentioned in the literature, which – like most cult-literature – concentrates single-mindedly on tenets of faith.

But then, I didn't think to ask him about it either – the Sage is, in his lightly abrasive way, quite compelling, and the interior of the house, with high-tech and low-tech, ancient and modern, all functioning together and looking rather well with it, is all part of the persona, so that you forget, for a time, that there is an outside, even though that is where all his carefully conserved energy has come from!

Tim Street-Porter
Travels with Banham

//

Reyner Banham
The Architecture of Silicon Valley

Published in *New West*, 22 September 1980, pp 47–51

Tim Street-Porter
Travels with Banham

I had studied architecture at the Regent Street Polytechnic during the mid-1960s, but never got to meet Peter Banham until much later – or even to glimpse him in traffic on his Moulton bike.

I never visited his domain at The Bartlett. My student activities brought me to the Architectural Association quite often, and I was invited to take part in events hosted by Peter Cook and other staff members there, befriending students and attending the fun annual AA carnival highlighted by the Bonzo Dog Doo-Dah Band.

I met Peter finally in 1980. I had moved to Los Angeles and was now a photographer, lured there by Frank Gehry, Ed Ruscha and other artists I had met on earlier visits, as well as by the visual attractions – the brilliant light, the palm trees and the desert landscapes. I was also primed by Banham's book on Los Angeles, which had given a new focus on the city and inspired a generation of European students to put the hitherto obscure LA on the map as a desirable and even necessary destination. Now well settled in the city I was hired to photograph the architecture of the newly burgeoning Silicon Valley for *New West* magazine.

The writer was Peter Banham, who very kindly invited me to stay overnight with his wife Mary at their home in nearby Santa Cruz. Thus we became friends. Two years later we did another magazine assignment together, this time documenting the impressive Daggett Solar Energy Plant in the Mojave Desert.

We met periodically in Los Angeles. He customarily stayed in Pasadena at the iconic Greene and Greene Gamble House, which impressed everyone. I had visions of him making toast in that wonderful kitchen. My wife Annie Kelly and I habitually lunched with him at the august, venerable Beaux Arts-style Biltmore Hotel in the Downtown, frequented in those days by conservative business and political fraternities. This was his choice – a little unexpected of someone so rooted in more modernistic habitats. We would meet in the vast lobby, little changed since 1923. An imposing figure, Peter always caused a minor stir when he walked in, dressed in his full Western regalia: hat, flourishing beard, bootlace tie, a hint of turquoise, jeans and cowboy boots. Onlookers must have assumed him to be a veteran actor from a nearby cowboy movie set, contradicted only by his broad Norfolk accent, which he did nothing to disguise, even to the maître d'.

Peter was a delightful and bracing companion. Annie and I were constantly dazzled by the sharpness of his intellect and total recall. We learned that when he produced an article he usually just typed it out from start to finish, without alterations. We attended one of his lectures, which he delivered with great flourish, unfailing eloquence and without notes.

I was very excited to be invited to join him on the trip he made around the wonderful and often surreal Mojave Desert to illustrate his *Scenes in America Deserta* book. We spent several days in his van in the beautiful winter light, all quite fabulous, and I was privileged to have him as guide and companion. When we reached the flat and smooth Silurian Dry Lake he extracted his faithful Moulton bike, which had been lurking without comment in the back of the van and announced casually that he always wanted to take a ride in the desert. This resulted in a perfect photographic moment, caught spontaneously. Whether he had quietly planned this I've still no idea!

Reyner Banham with his Moulton bicycle and Tim Street-Porter on Silurian Dry Lake in Death Valley, California, 1980.

Reyner Banham on the road in the Mojave Desert, California, captured by Tim Street-Porter, 1980.

REYNER BANHAM
THE ARCHITECTURE OF SILICON VALLEY:
THE BASIC BLACK BOX AND THE FIG LEAF BUSH

Neat, silvery smooth and as slickly styled as an advanced computer, IBM Corporation's Santa Teresa laboratory complex sits among ranch lands and orchards in the shelter of a ring of rounded, sun-dappled, yellow-grass hills that are so far south of the normally understood limits of Silicon Valley that the next stop down the highway must be Gilroy, the garlic capital of America.

It looks marvellous.

It is not only a geographical outpost of the electronic avant-garde, it is the epitome of the corporate vision that typifies the now legendary and world-renowned Silicon Valley. The valley is not simply a geographical location (running from Palo Alto through Santa Clara and San Jose to, so far, Santa Teresa), but a kind of heightened industrial consciousness based on the seemingly unlimited market for spiffy gadgetry derived from the silicon-chip microprocessor that has given you everything from credit card-size calculators to those habit-forming *Space Invader* games in penny arcades.

Palo Alto is where it all started, in the Stanford Industrial Park that now forms the northern tip of the Fertile Crescent of Electronics, close by the laboratories that gave us the very first transistors and the very first transistor-based companies; like Varian Associates, which is practically on the campus, and Hewlett-Packard a bit farther up the pike on Page Mill Road.

However, it is IBM, more than any other company, that developed the sharp, modern imagery that high-technology industries feel compelled to present to the public, and Santa Teresa is just about perfection of that kind – precise and elegant outwardly, almost an art gallery within, set in restrained, expensive and well-kept landscaping typified by lawns so neat they might as well be Astroturf.

The design, by the Berkeley-derived MBT Associates (the *M* stands for Gerald McCue, who is also the top architecture maven at Harvard), was commissioned in 1974. IBM's longtime design consultant and adviser was the late

Eliot Noyes, one of the founding good guys of better corporate imagery. The Eliot Noyes/Museum of Modern Art vision is everywhere in the Vale of Chips. Enter the front office of any typical company you care to name (its name, most likely, will be assembled from syllables such as 'syn', 'auto', 'tech', 'com' and 'ex'), and that vision will be all around you – colour-coordinated steel and plush furniture, limited-edition prints by the likes of Andy Warhol or posters from European art museums, an Indian pot or a great thingy in distressed macramé swarming down the wall behind the reception desk, a statuesque exotic plant or two, and wall-to-wall glass looking one way into a parking lot full of Porsches and the other way into a landscaped courtyard with a lump of stainless-steel sculpture in the middle. If you take comfort in the thought that glamour-stock companies are thriving and culturally aware, the valley can be a comforting place to be.

Or possibly not – there are a lot of FOR LEASE signs in the Vale of Chips right now. It may be the general economic malaise, or it may be something local, but whichever it is, this seems a good time to pause and take stock of the present state of corporate vision and high-tech architecture in the valley – and prompt upon the hour comes an exhibit opening September 2 at the San Jose Museum of Art under the appropriate title *Industrial Architecture in the Santa Clara Valley*. Organised by the Santa Clara Valley chapter of the American Institute of Architects, it aims to reveal the requirements, problems and successes of the special kind of architecture that grows in that Fertile Crescent.

It is a scene worth celebrating, because it adds up to a better-than-respectable body of architecture, even by world standards, and one of the more convincing regional styles practiced in the United States of late. Modern architecture knockers will immediately sneer that the style is international, not regional, and California mockers will equally as promptly point out that it isn't original and that they have seen better in Massachusetts, Switzerland or Japan. Such objections are both crass and unobservant. From the beginning, in the earliest buildings at Varian Associates, designed in 1953 by that great European exile, Erich Mendelsohn, there has been an elusive quality about even the most derivative Silicon Valley architecture that is special to the area and the industry. With the confidence born of success and regular three-for-two stock splitting, this is a mode of building that says: International-smashional, we're at home on our own turf.

If there is a benchmark building that sums up the basic style, it is Digital Equipment Corporation on Augustine Drive in Santa Clara, designed in 1976 by M Arthur Gensler and Associates, Inc, of San Francisco. It is the rock-bottom image, the ultimate black box: a rectangle of dark glass on a skinny plinth, standing on a mathematically precise plane of green lawn interrupted only by the lowercase logo – 'digital' – standing equally abstractly on its own skinny plinth. And that's it. Actually, if you go around to the side, you will see that the architects were prepared to compromise the box enough to make an entrance, but from most other viewpoints, the image is inviolate: a dark crystal on a green velvet mount.

From such a basic image, refined and absolute, the vision can be humanised, compromised, naturalised in any number of directions, but what is interesting and peculiarly Silicon Valley is the key role played by landscaping in these transformations – chiefly because there isn't much you can do about the box itself. Thus, at Alza Corporation (MBT Associates again, and Page Mill Road again) the box itself has been somewhat diversified by an exposed steel frame and brick panelling. But what really transforms the style is the well-grown timber that stands all around. The view from the back lawn in the evening, with the late, low sun picking out garden furniture and statuary between the long shadows of the trees across the grass, is more country house than high-tech. Anyone for croquet?

It's still the same basic box, however, whether you hang it with grids of steel sun shading, as at Fairchild Camera & Instrument Corporation in Mountain View, across the freeway from Moffet Field, or put a sexy kink in its mirrored façade, as at ADP Corporation next to Route 101 in Santa Clara. At its most nitty-grittily basic, it is the standard San Jose two-tone-avocado-with-racing-stripe tilt-up (so called because its plain concrete walls are cast flat on the ground and then tilted upright) that can currently be seen going up all over the valley, wherever energetic building entrepreneurs are trying to guess ahead of the coming demands for high-technology plants and high-quality warehousing.

A good place to see all this happening – currently, *the* place – is the International Business Park in northern San Jose, off the Montague Expressway. This sharp, well-promoted enterprise of the Mariani family (a name known to anyone who does business in the valley, from fruit to real estate) has high ambitions – just how high can be measured by the carefully contrived street address of the park's business office: 2001 Fortune Drive ('2001' as in *Space Odyssey*, 'Fortune' as in the top 500 companies and 'Drive' as in... libido?).

The same address also finds the park's chief commercial goody: an off-customs Foreign Trade Zone. It also has acres of basic tilt-ups, acres of well-kept landscaping, some internationally distinguished tenants (like Olympus Corporation) and at least one plant that is one of the architectural hot numbers of 1980, already featured in two top US architecture magazines and due for European and Japanese publication before the year is out.

This is Qume Corporation, designed in 1978 by John Duvivier of San Francisco (but at that time a member of Hawley and Peterson of Palo Alto), and it looks like the next benchmark building after Digital. It picks up most of the new themes in Silicon Valley architecture and makes a real smart package of them. Like your average tilt-up, it accepts the proposition that a façade is a front clipped onto the face of the box, a concept also accepted of late by top academic architects like Professor Charles Moore of UCLA, who, however, never seems to have as much fun with it as Duvivier does at Qume. Basically a set of overlapping flat screens in strong, no-nonsense colours, the façade is interrupted in the centre by a big red stair tower and, next to it, what appears to be the end of an even bigger pent-roof glass house, but at second-storey level.

Once inside you discover that the glass house (the glazing is insulating glass fibre material, in fact) is for real and that its pent roof runs back the full depth of this 240,000-square-foot plant, dividing it effectively into two parallel basic boxes with a mall in between. At the front end of this mall is the mandatory modern reception area, with artwork, fancy furniture and massively architected desk, but behind that runs a strip of closely planted *Ficus benjamina* and *Ficus ratusa*, with fountains and pools embracing the commissary and other areas. Buried among the shrubbery, for instance, you will find little clearings containing glass-top tables and blue-and-chrome chairs, where conclaves of workers will be discussing market strategy, foreign exchange and boyfriends or munching down sandwiches and drinking coffee, their heads just visible above the flat-trimmed top of the *benjamina*.

Internal greenery is accessible to the work force during break periods, is visible to nearly all of the workers as they toil at desk, bench or test rig and works on a scale more enormous than the mobile planters of dusty philodendron that lurk in other high-tech interiors. It could be a real breakthrough, a real expansion of the corporate vision of the valley. It has happened before and elsewhere, of course, but while Duvivier acknowledges the existence of internal gardens like that of the Ford Foundation in New York, the direct inspiration in this case came from the hanging ferns of Qume's earlier tilt-up in Hayward and the determination of one or two individuals inside the company to improve working conditions.

Other shifts of corporate vision can also be seen – canted roofs for solar panels, green terraces instead of roofs and an increasing tendency for newer buildings to try to look as if they were hiding underground. The most striking example of the new subterraneanism is Dysan Corporation (by Hill-Adams Associates, of Palo Alto) on Patrick Henry Drive in Santa Clara. It is low, with visibly pitched roofs pulled low over its eyes, so to speak. The line of the roofs is continued outward at all corners of the polygonal plan by massive struts whose lower ends are grounded in a chest-high earth bank that wraps almost completely around the building.

With the lowered eaves and the rising bank, those inside don't get much of a look at the world outside, but the bank itself is decently landscaped and filters a verdant light back into the building. The whole design clearly aims to make a strong public statement that this is a sensitive, energy-conscious, ecologically aware company, not a bunch of high-tech, high-energy show-offs such as some of the earlier denizens of the Vale of Chips are now deemed to be.

By their bush work shall ye know them. From the start, the historical development of the valley's corporate vision has been measured in shrubs and trees (Varian's earliest buildings

The impassive façades of Silicon Valley can absorb all sorts of exotica. Ricoh Systems, Inc, opened its San Jose plant with a Shinto ceremony. Too much happens too suddenly in the microchip business for anything to get very settled.

have been completely occluded by vegetation, for instance). Now that the function of planting has become more complex, sophisticated and integral to the total design, however, it begins to raise some old questions in new ways. Whom does the greenery benefit? Brave tries like Qume's aside, is it anything more than public relations – vegetable flack aimed at putting a new and less intimidating face on an industry whose links to power may not appeal to the current preferences for softer technology and a simpler society?

There are, however, a lot of rather fundamental aspects of the basic high-tech box that can't change very much. The need for a clean, well-lighted place to work is almost absolute. In the present state of industrial economics, that necessity means, almost unavoidably (and Dysan notwithstanding), rectangular, lightweight one- or two-story structures with big, clear spaces between skinny columns placed at infrequent intervals. It means a lot of light (usually artificial), air conditioning and other energy-consuming environmental gizmology (although careful design, as at Qume, can reduce the load noticeably). And it also means that a lot of the work force will be a long way from the comforts – and distractions – of outside views, regardless of how the windows are arranged.

But truth in architecture will out, sooner or later. Whatever the present preoccupation with external imagery and cosmetic shrubbery, it will need only a slight shift of corporate vision for the basic box to be found admirable for its simplicity and for Digital and IBM Santa Teresa to be praised for their naked honesty. For the moment, though, fig leaves are in, full frontal industrial nudity is out, and... how green is our Silicon Valley!

Qume Corporation's hard-edged, no-nonsense exterior masks a working space.

Qume Corporation's working space has been humanised with parklike greenery, fountains and pools.

The Architecture of Silicon Valley

Adrian Forty
Wordless in Zzyzx

//

Reyner Banham
The last pages of
Scenes in America Deserta

Published in *Scenes in America Deserta*, 1982, pp 220–8.

Adrian Forty
Wordless in Zzyzx

Critics aren't supposed to be lost for words. It seems like an admission of failure. Banham, who spent much of his life celebrating the new, in *Scenes in America Deserta* wrote about something that wasn't new at all, indeed a good deal older than humankind – the desert. This uncharacteristic shift of attention is accompanied by an equally uncharacteristic turnabout from his usual confidence in dealing with his subject matter. *Scenes in America Deserta* is the most personal of all Banham's books, and throughout the reader is conscious of his struggle to make sense of his experiences of the desert, to find a way to talk about it in ways other than in terms of the many images previous visitors have imposed upon it.

Coming at the very end of a book celebrating much that was strange about the desert, and his own self-discovery as a desert freak, the admission that ultimately he cannot say what enraptures him about it comes as a surprise. In place of the bravado of much of his earlier writing, he is assailed by doubt, by his own inadequacy to describe what he sees – and he admits it. He simply lacks the apparatus to turn the experience into language. It is one of the most honest, self-revealing admissions in all of Banham's writing. While he recognises the colours of the desert, unmoored as they appear from substance, to be analogous to some abstract painting – he refers to Helen Frankenthaler – at the time, he knows this comparison to be woefully inadequate, merely a product of his own visual training. Banham finds himself naked, utterly lacking terms to describe the very thing that has meant most to him. His respect grows for the early-20th-century writer John van Dyke, for having come so close to managing to do just this. But for himself, he is reduced to clichés – 'mystical', 'hallucinatory', 'beautiful' – and for a writer who spent his life scorning clichés, always searching for fresh metaphors, this is a humbling admission. The desert, it seems, defeated him – and he lets us know it.

REYNER BANHAM
The last pages of *SCENES IN AMERICA DESERTA*

All would confess a desire to return, almost uncontrollable in some cases. The desert, once seen, cannot be left alone if one has any feeling for it at all. To me, this seems fundamentally unlike one's response to scenes, perhaps equally beloved, in other landscapes and topographies. For instance, I love the little cities of central Italy – Cortona, Arezzo, Orvieto, Urbino. I would love to see Urbino again for the pleasures it affords all the senses – its heroic site; the seemingly inexhaustible pleasures of light and shade and sculptured stone in the enclosed courtyards of the Ducal Palace; the humanistic rhetoric, grave and precise, of the lettered friezes dedicated to the glorious memory of Duke Federico of Montefeltro; Piero della Francesca's *Flagellation*, most mysterious and studiedly stylish of all his paintings; that miraculous and most rewarding of visual jokes, the inlaid trompe-l'oeil woodwork of the Duke's *studiolo*, and that dazzling prospect of quintessential Italian countryside that strikes the eye when one steps out onto the balcony between the twin towers outside the *studiolo*. Wonderful... but I do not feel deprived of Urbino when I am away, as I might feel deprived of the view of Cima Dome from the first crest of Cedar Canyon Road, the mighty prospect of Death Valley from Dante's View, or the weathered turret-dome of sacred Baboquivari lording it over the lesser mountains south of Kitt Peak. In general, I feel deprived of the subtle visual effects: like the blown sand that wedges against the footings of the dry mountains throughout America Deserta, a light, white border that separates the mountain from the plain and insures that the mountain will be artfully graded in colour and tone from dark blue or brown where its crest line meets the sky to misty paleness at its base, bereft of substance and weight. The deprivations of absence from the deserts are always primarily visual. The desert is not, for me, freedom, adventure, refuge, or escape, nor even the illusions thereof. It does not offer me material rewards of cash or kind. The rewards of the desert are in the eye of the beholder, they are patterns on the rods and cones of the retinas of the eyes that deliver messages to the visual cortex of the brain, and the brain finds them as puzzling as they are exhilarating, because they seem to signal something I had not deemed possible in myself – a pure aesthetic response.

//

Deprived of the ancient categories of Picturesque and Sublime; dubious as to whether the deserts may be Beautiful in any equally ancient sense; knowing that I came into America Deserta culturally naked and ill-prepared; aware that I return to these landscapes in order to feast my eyes on visions that I am prepared to term addictive; I find myself driven closer than ever in my life to the idea that some scenes may be perceived as, simply, 'beautiful' – that the unthinking desert layabouts who say that 'it just is' may be on to something real. There does seem to be something out there that communicates more directly to the pleasure centres of my brain than anything else I have ever encountered.

And I think that surprising something is, after all, a matter of colour and light. As visual compositions, the scenes of the deserts of the American West are rarely commanding or intriguing in themselves, once one has subtracted the inevitable fascinations of human tracks and traces on the land. I had toyed with the idea that the desert's simple confrontations of horizontal and vertical, and the broad washes of tone and texture, might have evoked something of the iconographies of abstract art. And that is still a possibility I am reluctant to let go – largely because those abstract iconographies represent styles of seeing which are extremely familiar, even emotionally effective, to myself and most of my generation. It is not difficult to make a Mondrian out of some deserts; a Jackson Pollock out of others; and one or two abstract painters like Helen Frankenthaler have done extremely effective pieces in which not one single representation element can be distinguished, yet they are totally permeated with the sense of the desert.

Pictures like that (her *Indian Redscape*, for instance) leave me even more profoundly suspecting that it is colour – which is about all that the picture contains – and light – which the picture everywhere implies – that are the true contents of whatever it is that gets into my eyes in American deserts. This, assuredly, is what recommended John van Dyke to me at the very first reading of the first page opened at random. Whatever else may be great in van Dyke, and whatever may be wrong with him to make the book a 'flawed masterpiece', it is his obsessive, impassioned attention to the exact description of light and its fractured offspring, the colours of the spectrum, which commands my attention.

There is one passage that seems to come very close to the kernel of the matter, at least as it affects me. It is about the colour of sand in the desert.

'The sands are not golden, except under peculiar circumstances, such as when they are whirled high in the air by the winds and then struck broadside by the sunlight. Lying quietly upon the earth they are usually dull yellow. In the morning light they are often grey, at noon frequently a bleached yellow, and at sunset occasionally pink or saffron-hued. Wavering heat and mirage give them temporary colouring at times that is beautifully unreal. They then appear to undulate slightly like the smooth surface of the summer sea at sunset; and the colours shift and travel with the undulations.'

At first reading, this passage – so ethereal, so concerned with the 'visible world' and nothing else, seemed to epitomise the art-for-art's-sake, the pure aestheticism of van Dyke. After all, he was of Roger Fry's generation, and would therefore be preoccupied with the abstract and insubstantial qualities of art; and I remembered the story of Roger Fry lecturing for an hour on a Crucifixion in the National Gallery in London and never referring to the suffering figure on the cross as anything but 'the main central mass of colour'! It would be in the style of his period to ignore people in the desert and concentrate on purely visual matters. But on re-reading van Dyke as I got to know the Southwest better, my estimation began to change from 'What else would you expect him to write about?' to 'What else was there for him to write about?'

I now suspect that much of his power comes from his rightness in time and place, author and subject entirely appropriate to one another, an abstract landscape meeting an aesthete who was more of an abstractionist than he himself may have suspected, and coming together in a fusion of vision and words focused upon that most crucial of desert observations: the apparent separation of colour from substance, the replacement of light reflected by solid bodies by light refracted near the surfaces of those bodies and the appearance of colour in the space between the solid bodies. Van Dyke's insistence on the 'coloured air' of the desert depends on a very truthful observation of a visible fact, even if his physical explanations are sometimes dubious. At morning, but even more in the late afternoon, colour seems to emanate as light throughout the atmosphere, dissolving solids, confusing distances, modifying local colours almost out of recognition. For instance, I remember the deserts of California and Arizona as blue deserts in contrast to the red deserts of Four Corners country, but this is almost pure illusion; the local colours in the earth and rocks are white and brown and grey and often tawny red, but the air between blues them all. The refracting air layer and crackle pattern of the surface of a salt lake will make it look dark chocolate brown against the sun, and silver-blue looking the other way, producing a curiously dizzying effect as one turns around on the lake surface.

Now although I am loath to share the physiological determinist's view that certain colours reliably provoke certain fixed cerebral responses (the old red-rag-to-a-bull legend) because the evidence advanced normally ignores matters like the context and associations of the forms in which the colours are presented, I have to admit that here in America Deserta one may see colour as nearly divorced from substance and context, colour as light, as anywhere outside a hologram laboratory. And that kind of colour, I think, gets under my guard, that kind of light seems to go more nearly straight through my eye than anything else I have seen anywhere in the world. These may be the purest responses to colour and light I have ever made in my adult life, or they may be among the most impure and complex – for just at the point where I believed I had discovered an unmediated aesthetic response in myself, I began to suspect the presence of something else. These dissociations of colour and light might, perhaps, have other appeals and stir other responses, not all of them simplistically pleasurable.

It is, of course, the kind of colour and light that most of us have been privileged to enjoy at occasional sunrises and sunsets all over the world. But to have it all around, all day, to see it between ourselves and all solid objects – even the very ground at our feet, as van Dyke records in his observation of sand colours – and to be able to avoid it only at dawn (which is often the least coloured part of the day, once the green glow has passed)... such an omnipresence of coloured light, brilliant, raw, subtle or hallucinatory, may be almost too much for our sensibilities to handle, especially if we come from the veiled greyer atmospheres of Northern Europe.

Indeed, one might wonder if we take cover behind the sunglasses of our technological culture, not simply because the light is strong and threatens to hurt our eyes, but because the light is so extreme, and the independence of colour and form so unsettling, that it somehow threatens our established psychologies as well, and evokes uninvited responses with a directness that is difficult to bear. Whatever these psychological effects may be, they have not much to do with beauty as traditionally understood, neither in the eighteenth century sense of forms 'smooth, gentle, rounded, feminine' nor in the senses in which Plato originally codified the concept of beauty – functional appropriateness in the *Greater Hippias*, and abstract mathematical geometry of the famous definition of absolute beauty in the *Philebus* – because all these understandings of Beauty involve the concept of pleasure and the one thing the disembodied light and colour of the desert are not – solid objects.

Consistently, Plato – so good on solids – is disappointing on colour and, to my mind, dull on light. Perhaps they were too much for his sensibilities as well; he is notably wary of anything that might disturb his orderly constructs, much as he was wary of the havoc that poets might work on the solid body of his Republic. For disembodied light, without an identifiable source of radiation, is always unsettling – the false light of the Will-o'-the-Wisp, the soaring curtains of the Aurora Borealis, and the prevalence of disembodied lights and colours in mystical experiences and hallucinations. Or could it be that words like mystical and hallucinatory are convenient labels with which to categorise, and thus tame, responses that were not tame, and far outside the categories of common physical experience? And that to call the light and colour of the desert beautiful, is just another tame category for experiences that are seemingly beyond our reasonable expectations of how the world should appear?

'The clear light of day' is such a frequent metaphor for the rational operations of the logical mind that to find light subverting reason is bound to be unsettling. But it seems to me that the manner in which the disembodied colour and unfocused light of the desert subvert reason is so provocative that it is worth a paragraph's reflection.

It was that painting by Helen Frankenthaler that gave me a clue to what might be happening, and might explain at least part of the reason for the desert's visual impact upon me. It is a painting of disembodied colour, and of very little else – yet it is all desert. In its divorce of colour from objects and forms, it separates what is normally only a contingent attribute (the colour red) from the solids to which in normal life it is firmly anchored. In other words it performs, or mocks, one of the crucial operations of abstract reasoning, by which we can verbally isolate the attribute red from the physical noun to which it normally belongs. And notice how the punning title celebrates this dislocation – *Indian Redscape* – even if the pigment name *Indian Red* is now known only to an older generation of painters.

Few of us in our daily round will ever see adjectives separated from nouns in this way; we see red tomatoes and green apples and yellow bananas. But we don't see the colours apart from the fruits; and it took a long time for even the most sophisticated men of antiquity to be able to make much verbal discrimination between colours – the poverty of colour words in Greek, even as late as Plato, is now almost proverbial and makes us wonder how many colours they could even visually discriminate.

So the disembodied colours that haunt (we have no other word for it) the desert eerily short-circuit a process of reasoned discrimination that has cost Western Man long centuries of verbal exercise of the faculty of reason. But in making her particular celebration of this short circuit, Helen Frankenthaler is also drawing on respectable traditions in Modern Art since about the time of the post-Impressionists. Colour and form have long been two separable topics of painterly discourse – often within the terms of a single painting – from the dislocations of early Cubism to the final efflorescence of colour-field painting in the 1950s.

That is why I am still unwilling to give up the idea that there may be some congruence between the look of the deserts and some abstract art; but I cannot advance this idea in the comforting and reassuring guise of an iconography that I learned in youth or as a student of art history. The whole matter is too appropriately tenuous for that, and in many ways my responses are too strong to be so neatly explained. However, it was somewhat reassuring that this particular train of thought should have been opened up by a work of art, for *Indian Redscape* is a fine and commanding painting that would probably have stuck in my visual memory anyhow. And it is bound to gratify one's vanity if one finds that the preoccupations of the day are answered by major works, rather than no account trivia.

For the desert is not trivial. Even if one only skitters across its surface in leisure clothes and casual shoes, even if every night's destination is a surprise-free franchised motel, there is still something large and mysterious about the experience of being in it. The first old-timer with whom I ever swapped value judgments about the Mojave phrased it thus:

'Ah love thuh Desert. Used to live on thuh Coast, work for thuh State of California, got muhself transferred up here. Wouldn't move 'way agin. Ain't no two ways 'bout it: yuh either loves the desert or yuh hates it... Ah love it!'

Every move, every gesture, every facial expression, every turn of phrase suggested role playing – even the accent sounded acquired. Yet I know (from what I learned about him later) that he was not codding me, nor codding himself. If you love anything as fundamentally inhospitable to the lazy and self-indulgent human race as a desert, then you may well have credibility problems, even within yourself. It may be a necessary support and comfort to adopt a guise that has been codified and sanctified by art (if only the movies) and speak through a persona that seems more appropriate than one's own.

Behind the play-acting, however, I think there was truth. There are no two ways about the desert; there are no middle opinions; and I have never met anyone who was just a 'mild' desert lover. And it could be that the old-timer's B-movie prose was a way of controlling responses that surprised him as much as mine had already surprised me, for this was already my second visit to the Mojave and I knew that I was in over my ears committed and out of my depth.

And something of my long-term uneasiness and fascination with the desert derives, I suspect, from my never having found a suitable disguise or function with which to designate my relationship to this landscape I love. I feel sure that if I could be a professional old-timer, a Ranger for the BLM[1], or the line man who services the telephone that rejoices in the call number Landfair 1, I could be able to use words like *beautiful* without wondering what I mean by them, and how I came by the responses that drive me to use words like that.

Clearly, the desert has done to me what it has done to many of us desert freaks – it has made me ask questions about myself that I would never otherwise have asked. And since I have no convincing answers to those questions (*Indian Redscape* is only a clue, not an answer), I have not done what one has been supposed to do in deserts ever since the time of Moses – I have not 'found myself'. If anything I have lost myself, in the sense that I now feel that I understand myself less than I did before.

What I have truly found, however, is something that I value, in some ways, more than myself. Beauty may indeed lie in the eye of the beholder, but that eye must have an object of vision, a scene on which it can fasten, and I have found that scene, and appropriate objects of scrutiny within it, and that light and that colour. And all this I knew (I believe) from the very moment that my eye was taken by the vision of that ethereal luminous mist on that first morning in the Mojave. The desert hath me in thrall, and I am happy to say that I am still astonished to discover that this is so.

---

1 [Referring here to the United States Bureau of Land Management.]

Ludovico Centis
A Farewell to Words

//

Reyner Banham
The Wall

Published in *SAH Newsletter*, no 6, 1994, pp 9–10.

Ludovico Centis
A Farewell to Words

'This dumb wall.' These are the last three words written by Peter Reyner Banham, typed in a hospital bed in mid-March 1988. Being stuck in a room for months as a consequence of treatment for cancer is indeed a dreadful condition. Even more so for a man who was particularly fond of wide-open spaces, whether Mousehold Heath on the outskirts of Norwich which he explored in his youth, the shores of Lake Erie to which he often escaped to contemplate the sunset in Upstate New York or the desert landscapes of the American West that he repeatedly traversed and to which he devoted his most intimate book, *Scenes in America Deserta*.

    Despite his precarious health, Banham continued to be a sharp writer. While he couldn't literally reach through the wall with his whole arm, as he happened to do while exploring a grain elevator in Silo City in Buffalo, NY, the initial lines of the text are dedicated to a detailed description of the visible and invisible features of the wall: the birthday cards, the stuccoed surface and most importantly the leaf of lead that – while shielding him from the radiation deriving from the nearby radiology treatments – constituted an even more impenetrable barrier for his dreams of escape.

    Banham's attention then shifts from the room to a bitter list of missed opportunities. First of all 'Actual Monuments', the never-delivered inaugural lecture to be debuted on the occasion of his taking up of the Sheldon H Solow Chair for the History of Architecture at the Institute of Fine Arts, New York University. Then, the annual meeting of the Society of Architectural Historians in Chicago, where he would have come across a diverse set of characters that he depicts with benevolent sarcasm. He ends with a list of travel destinations, some more exotic than others.

If 'Actual Monuments' can be considered Banham's last public testament (though not intended as such), 'The Wall' – and in particular its closing lines – stands out as his private, intimate one. Not for obvious reasons – that it is the last text he wrote in a stunningly prolific career – but for the clarity and strength of the 'we' that he evoked. The 'we' that meant Peter and Mary. The 'we' that generated a family and that engaged relentlessly with architecture, both as built heritage and as a community of practitioners, scholars and students. It is with this overt tribute to and recognition of the person who made his whole career possible and meaningful that Peter Reyner Banham gave his farewell to words. And forget the dumb wall.

REYNER BANHAM
THE WALL

At the foot of the bed is this wall, currently covered in sixty-sixth birthday cards, but otherwise a regular stuccoed interior partition in a regular modern-style hospital. Only it isn't... that wall has extra substance, both physically and psychologically – a leaf of lead allegedly half an inch thick, wall to wall and floor to ceiling. That's very reassuring, because the room on the other side is one of the 'hot rooms' for radiology patients to relapse in after/during treatment.

But it is also very daunting at one particular symbolic juncture – my own! If this bed were a vehicle of dreams – such as it still is on good nights when the isomorphine is benign – then monster wall blocks all forward travel; there isn't going to be a Banham programme of activities this year, not in New York, nor in Continental Europe, and above all, not in Chicago.

This was the bitterest blow of all – I sat there in the bed-that-ain't-going-nowhere with the prospectus of the 1988 Convention of the Society of Architectural Historians in my hand, staring at that dumb wall – and, inexorably, the tears began to trickle between my lids.

Officially, and ceremonially, the peak of the year was already past, of course – the inaugural lecture that I should have given at the Institute of Fine Arts. But Chicago/SAH would have been our annual re-baptism in the warm, nutritious fluids and friendships of our trade. There was the whole sweep of the four-day proceedings, which – in a self-consciously architectural city like Chicago – can get so clotted and overwrought that some speakers almost miss their sessions because they have become totally engrossed in something totally different.

One or two papers really are as important as that, but most of them are old friends performing new marvels with material they have possessed as long as we have known them, others will be former students scratching in the corners of their lunch-pails of information that they brought with them from home. Some will be world-experts of very *haut mien*; others will be lovable bundles of provincial fun, securely wrapped around archival information that will only be released in their wills.

But the real point is that we have known some of them for decades – and even if some of them are charlatans and speakers with divided tongues – they are still the basis of the largest community to which we have ever consciously contributed. That is the bit that really hurts, and it comes as a surprise to me.

For some time I had been making a kind of negative serendipity list of things that it might have been rather gratifying to do or do again given half a chance – go up to Machu Picchu in the Andes, slip down into a well-concealed fishing hole in the bank of the Wiltshire Avon on a July afternoon to smell what a properly matured and productive river looks like, go to Urbino, for the sake of that view from the balconies of the *studiolo*, hooking my nose over the brim of a heavy duty Barossa Red in the late cooling of those luminous South-Australian afternoons.

Idle pipe-dreams, plastic drain-pipe dreams driven by the fact that I have not partaken normally of food for three months now. Adaptation to a foodless diet was less of a hassle than I had expected – Force Bloody Majeure, Man! – or do you want to spend the rest of your life puking up eighteen hundred ccs of roiling green blue bile, every night upon the very midnight clear?

Topographical fast-forward ought to be easier to manage, since it contains so little of direct human substance, and can hardly make you puke! Perhaps it's all too aesthetical, too commercialised. But it can be pushed aside... and in any case, this bed isn't going to penetrate that wall, is it? Leaving me mourning the one topographical fast-forward that isn't an idle pipe-dream but one that we could still just about afford if we weren't still in the United States and in employment... and – HEEEYYY!! – just look at those second person plural pronouns in that last sentence there, affirming the continuing 'WE' of the Banhams, who have never done the Society of Architectural Historians apart, always together. Always as an outlet for our love of the subject that we love almost as much as our off-spring: Debby, Ben, Olly, Mary, Architecture – what are you doing on the other side of this dumb wall.

Oliver Arditi
The Elision of Geography

I once spent an afternoon with my grandparents, Mary and Peter Reyner Banham, in the deep, lush back garden belonging to one of their friends in Los Angeles. The only memory I have of the conversation is their friend's casual racism, directed at a Black plumber who had recently worked in their house, and the uncomfortable 'ah...' my grandfather gave in response.

That mute 'ah...' is perhaps emblematic of Banham's relationship with the US and its stark inequalities. He was a European socialist intellectual who lived through the privations of the Depression, the Second World War and the following years of austerity. He was not at all aligned to the political values that informed the American way of life or its material culture, but he loved the place, and especially the experiences afforded by its disposable consumerism. He gave positive valuations to Los Angeles' car-centred mass cultural artefacts – the freeways, the roadside diners and the automobiles themselves – as works of design, demonstrating an unconventional conviction that such objects should be valued as the exemplary aesthetic representatives of their cultural and historical circumstances. But of the steep gradients of inequality that make the American Dream accessible to some, he had very little to say. I certainly wouldn't suggest that the social deprivation suffered in large parts of the urban US invalidate the point that Banham reiterated throughout his career: that so-called 'low culture' should be understood and valued on its own terms. But clearly Banham either couldn't find the language to acknowledge both sides of that coin, or felt that it was not his job to do so.

In *Los Angeles: The Architecture of Four Ecologies*, he makes some reference to 'problem areas' such as Watts, discussing the flat, valley-bottom street grids that he refers to as 'the great plains of Id' as a 'service area supplying the foothills and beaches'. He examines the role that unscrupulous property developers played in shaping the area, and even mentions the Watts riots of 1965, but nowhere does he seem to acknowledge race or class as structural factors in the composition or dynamics of Los Angeles. The book has been fairly criticised for this elision – a slip which appears to be paralleled in the ways that Banham's Angelenos experience their city. Other than this observation though, I'm barely capable of reading it critically. Not only does it embody the voice of a man I love and miss (and Banham's informal spoken voice can always be heard in his prose by those who knew him), but I don't know nearly enough about LA or architectural history. In his *Los Angeles Times* review of the 2009 edition, Richard Rayner notes Banham's avoidance of sources that took a darker view of Southern California than he, and concludes that 'most likely Banham didn't want to go there. [...] Banham wrote like a blissed-out lover, surrendering to his feelings of derangement and wonder while keeping his eyes wide-open.'

That's a phrase that puts me in mind of writers like Tom Wolfe and Hunter S Thompson, whose New Journalism techniques I know Banham admired, and which I think can be seen at work in *Los Angeles*. In Banham's decision to 'learn to drive in order to read Los Angeles in the original' there is a parallel to the immersion practiced in New Journalism; in a similar manner to Wolfe, Banham also chose to spend time living among Angelenos, as an Angeleno, in order to decipher the most exciting and culturally distant urban text he had yet encountered. His book was also a deliberate attempt to upset the conventions and assumptions of architectural history writing, formally and methodologically: the book's organisation around the four ecologies of his title is clearly an act of revolt against conventional architectural history narratives, which tended to fabulate a linear sequence of foundation and development, the construction of important buildings and their influence on important architects. The multiple loci of Banham's narrative render the city's history resistant to the usual hierarchies of time and influence, and indeed to those of geographic centrality and peripherality.

The freeways, which he presents as equivalent to the totality of other metropolises' great churches, museums, civic buildings, palaces and whatever-the-hell-else, are formally beautiful to Banham, but properly consumed at the wheel of a car. The intersection of the Santa Monica and San Diego freeways 'is a work of art, both as pattern on the map, a monument against the sky and as a kinetic experience as one sweeps through it', but the book makes clear that it is the last that is privileged. Whether it is its aesthetics, its sociality, its topography or its history, for Banham Los Angeles is correctly apprehended in a movement *through*; the experience of living there is one of motility, of eliding the geographic distance between wherever you are now and whatever it is you need to do next.

Maristella Casciato
Afterword: Reyner Banham Then and Now

This book is not a straightforward anthology of texts; not a chronological itinerary through Banham's long-active career nor a comprehensive view of his nomadic interests. It is rather a generative venture, rooted as much in the present as in the past; one which acknowledges the continual reverberations of Banham's writing more than three decades after his death in 1988.

The publication emerges from an exercise in which the editor selected a group of generationally diverse scholars, invited them to choose any passage from the English historian's work and to critically reread their chosen excerpt. This intellectual frame produced a surprising result, where six of the fourteen contributions refer to only two books out of Banham's considerable oeuvre,[1] namely *Los Angeles: The Architecture of Four Ecologies* (1971) and *Scenes in America Deserta* (1982).[2] Even though selection is always an act of obliteration of some aspects, the density of interest in these books – both of which show the author's deep fascination with the environmental cacophony of southern California – seems to say something of the lens through which Banham's thoughts, ideas and premises are evaluated and appropriated *now*.

In its first instance, *Los Angeles: The Architecture of Four Ecologies* was meant to shed light onto the *weltanschauung* of Los Angeles' idiosyncratic urbanity, with Banham's outlook running counter to the negative views of Los Angeles' urban condition at the time. It is certainly a fact that this original impulse to contrast the mainstream of modern architecture, which animated Banham *then*, has now turned to a stage in which his anti-bourgeois and transgressive responses have been assimilated into a global neoliberal order. The intellectual genesis of the book is revealed in Banham's epigraph, in which he acknowledges architect Cedric Price – 'who first called upon [him] to testify in public on LA'.[3] In his career as a designer and educator, Price had made it clear that what interested him was not objects but processes, in this sense paving the way for what the subtitle of Banham's volume suggested. The triangulation between Price, Banham and Los Angeles captures the unorthodox narrative Banham puts forward in his table of contents: the four ecologies are introduced in parallel with as many reflections on and for architecture, and are interspersed with annotations that follow a lexicon built on a palimpsest of cinematic imageries. Banham is learning directly from Los Angeles.

The historian Anthony Vidler offers another temporal dimension to the four ecologies through the title of his thoughtful introduction to the 2001 edition of the book, portraying Los Angeles as the city of the 'immediate future' in an attempt to highlight Banham's pursuit of a better tomorrow.[4] Vidler's examination of the narrative structure of the book is particularly noteworthy, as he aims to demonstrate the 'development of Banham's thoughts as a historian rather than the "journalist"' and to create a lineage with the notable German architectural historian Nikolaus Pevsner, Banham's tutor. Eventually, Vidler notes that in *Theory and Design in the First Machine Age* (1960)[5] and similarly in his creative tale around the four ecologies, Banham interpreted modernity as the expression of movement and of mechanised technologies: as a steady and unquestionable trajectory, both metaphorically and mechanically. In highlighting Banham's development and lineage alongside his aesthetic philosophy, Vidler reconnects the *then* and the *now*, ie the architectural culture in London in the late 1950s and 60s and the allure of the extended pop fantasies of Los Angeles, expanding this genealogy to incorporate the environmental experience of 'America deserta'. Among the many tracks this book touches upon, from the digital turn to the lure of concrete, from technology to materials, I wish to add one more which plays off this apparent contemporary focus on the Southwest United States and establishes bonds between Banham's views of Los Angeles and the works of Ed Ruscha (exhibited, at the time of writing, in a retrospective at LACMA).[6] These two adopted citizens of the low-density, highly dispersed urban conglomeration of Los Angeles became close friends and their explorative imaginations created multiple connections.[7] If traces of pop culture became the signature of the four ecologies, later visualised in the BBC documentary *Reyner Banham Loves Los Angeles* (1972), Ed Ruscha's rich fascination for gasoline stations, parking lots, freeways, interchanges, billboards, palm trees and decorative sheds fabricated more musical movements to accompany the same sonata.

1   See 'Bibliography', in *A Critic Writes: Selected Essays by Reyner Banham*, edited by Mary Banham, Paul Barker, Sutherland Lyall and Cedric Price (University of California Press, 1996), pp 301–36.
2   I have taken the liberty of associating the American deserts with the contribution by British photographer Tim Street-Porter, with whom Banham traveled through the magical solitude of the Mojave Desert and beyond.
3   Reyner Banham, *Los Angeles: The Architecture of Four Ecologies* (Penguin, 1971), p 5.
4   Anthony Vidler, 'Los Angeles: City of the Immediate Future', in Reyner Banham, *Los Angeles: The Architecture of Four Ecologies* (University of California Press, 2001), p xxi.
5   Reyner Banham, *Theory and Design in the First Machine Age* (The Architectural Press, 1960). The title of the book is eponymous to that of Banham's dissertation.
6   *ED RUSCHA / NOW THEN*, exhibition at the Los Angeles County Museum of Art (LACMA), 7 April–6 October 2024.
7   Ludovico Centis in conversation with Ed Ruscha, 'Where the city meets the desert', in *AA Files* 77, Autumn/Winter 2020, pp 78–84.

Biographies

Oliver Arditi

Oliver Arditi was born in 1970 to Reyner Banham's daughter Debby. Since leaving home on a whim at the age of 17, he has been an agricultural labourer, gallery technician, musician, nursery teacher, conservation technician, librarian and writer. He lives in rural Suffolk with his wife Liz, and, until recently, his daughter Lucy. He spends his time working in a small library and building unfeasibly detailed fantasy worlds.

Mario Carpo

Mario Carpo is Reyner Banham Professor of Architectural History and Theory at The Bartlett School of Architecture (UCL). His research and publications focus on the history of early modern architecture, and on the theory and criticism of contemporary design and technology. His books include *Architecture in the Age of Printing* (2001), which has been translated into several languages; *The Alphabet and the Algorithm* (2011); *The Second Digital Turn: Design Beyond Intelligence* (2017); and *Beyond Digital. Design and Automation at the End of Modernity* (2023), all published by MIT Press.

Maristella Casciato

Maristella Casciato is senior curator and head of architectural collections at the Getty Research Institute in Los Angeles, where she has co-curated exhibitions including *The Metropolis in Latin America, 1830–1930* (2017), *MONUMENT(ALITY)* (2018) and *Bauhaus Beginnings* (2019). Among her recent publications are *Rethinking Global Modernism* (co-edited with Vikramaditya Prakash and Daniel E Coslett, 2022), *Technoscape* (co-edited with Pippo Ciorra, 2022) and the facsimile reprint of *Le Corbusier Album Punjab, 1951* (2024). Casciato has been nominated 2023 Fellow of the Society of Architectural Historians.

Ludovico Centis

Ludovico Centis is an architect, founder of the office The Empire and cofounder and editor of the architecture magazine *San Rocco*. He is currently Assistant Professor in Urbanism at the University of Trieste. His research focuses on the ways individuals and institutions, as well as desires and power, shape cities and landscapes. Centis has been the 2013–14 Peter Reyner Banham Fellow at the State University of New York at Buffalo. Recent books include *The Lake of Venice. A Scenario for Venice and its Lagoon* (co-authored with Lorenzo Fabian, 2022), *They Must Have Enjoyed Building Here: Reyner Banham and Buffalo* (2021) and *A Parallel of Ruins and Landscapes* (2019).

Adrian Forty

Adrian Forty is Professor Emeritus of Architectural History at the Bartlett School of Architecture (UCL) and Honorary Curator of Architecture at the Royal Academy of Arts, London. He is the author of *Objects of Desire, Design and Society Since 1750* (1986); *Words and Buildings, a Vocabulary of Modern Architecture* (2000); *Concrete and Culture, a Material History* (2012) and, most recently, with Barbara Penner, Olivia Horsfall Turner and Miranda Critchley, *Extinct. A Compendium of Obsolete Objects* (2021).

Curt Gambetta

Curt Gambetta is a postdoctoral fellow in the Dartmouth College Society of Fellows and a lecturer in the Department of Art History at Dartmouth. Previously, he was a Visiting Critic at the Cornell University School of Architecture, Art and Planning (2021–23), the Peter Reyner Banham Fellow at the University at Buffalo School of Architecture and Planning (2011–12) and a teaching fellow at Woodbury University in Los Angeles (2012–13). His current book projects centre on histories of fieldwork in the built environment and the politics of building materials in postcolonial India.

Kersten Geers

Kersten Geers is an architect, writer and educator. With David Van Severen he is a founding partner of the Brussels-based architecture firm OFFICE Kersten Geers David Van Severen. Geers has taught at institutions including the Berlage Institute, Columbia University (GSAPP), Yale School of Architecture, Harvard University (GSD) and EPF Lausanne. He currently holds a professorship at the Academy of Architecture in Mendrisio. Geers was a founding editor of the architecture magazine *San Rocco*, and some of his recent books are *Without Content* (2021), *Excess of Architecture* (2022) and *Experiments in Thickness* (2023).

Albert Narath

Albert Narath is a historian of the built environment whose current research focuses on the intersection of architectural and environmental history from the 18th century to the present. His book *Solar Adobe: Energy, Ecology, and Earthen Architecture* (2024) focuses on the emergence of a 'solar adobe' design scene in the American Southwest following the Second World War, when debates about ecology and technology were central. Narath is Associate Professor in the History of Art and Visual Culture Department at the University of California, Santa Cruz, where Banham taught from 1980 to 1987.

Barbara Penner

Barbara Penner is Professor in Architectural Humanities at The Bartlett School of Architecture (UCL). She is author of *Bathroom* (2013), which was awarded the 2014 RIBA President's Award for Outstanding University-Located Research, and *Newlyweds on Tour: Honeymooning in Nineteenth-Century America* (2009). She is co-editor of *Extinct: A Compendium of Obsolete Objects* (2021), *Sexuality and Gender at Home* (2017), *Ladies and Gents: Public Toilets and Gender* (2009), and *Gender Space Architecture* (2000). She is a contributing editor to the online architecture journal *Places*, for which she wrote an appreciation of Reyner Banham, 'The Man who Wrote Too Well' (2015).

Penny Sparke

Penny Sparke is Professor of Design History at Kingston University and the director of the Modern Interiors Research Centre. She taught the history of design at Brighton Polytechnic (1975–82) and the Royal College of Art (1982–99). She was Dean of the Faculty of Art, Design and Music at Kingston University from 1999 to 2005 and Pro Vice-Chancellor from 2005 to 2014. Her publications include *An Introduction to Design and Culture, 1900 to the present* (1986 and 2004); *Italian Design from 1860 to the present* (1989); *As Long as It's Pink: The Sexual Politics of Taste* (1995); *The Modern Interior* (2008); and *Nature Inside: Plants and Flowers in the Modern Interior* (2021).

Tim Street-Porter

Tim Street-Porter is an architecture and design photographer and author. He has worked for most of the design magazines in the US, including *Architectural Digest*, *Elle Décor* and *Vanity Fair*. He has written and photographed more than ten books on design and architecture, including *Los Angeles* (2005), *LA Modern* (2008) and *Palm Springs: A Modernist Paradise* (2018). He has also photographed a series of books with his writer/designer wife Annie Kelly, the most recent of which are *Los Angeles Today: City of Dreams* (2021) and their new book *City of Dreams: Los Angeles Interiors* (2024).

Alice Twemlow
Alice Twemlow is Professor in the Wim Crouwel Chair of the History of Graphic Design and Visual Culture at the University of Amsterdam and a Research Professor at the Royal Academy of Art (KABK) The Hague. She cofounded and directed the MA in Design Criticism at the School of Visual Arts in New York. She has a PhD in History of Design from the Royal College of Art (RCA), and her book, *Sifting the Trash: A History of Design Criticism*, was published by MIT Press in 2017.

Paola Viganò
Paola Viganò is an architect and urbanist, as well as Full Professor in Urban Theory and Urban Design at the EPFL Lausanne where she directs the Habitat Research Centre and the Laboratory of Urbanism; she is also Professor at IUAV University of Venice. She cofounded Studio Bernardo Secchi-Paola Viganò (1990–2014), and since 2015 has run StudioPaolaViganò, a practice that focuses on the ecological and social transition of cities, landscapes and territories. Her latest book is *The Biopolitical Garden. Space, Life, Transition* (2024).

Richard J Williams
Richard J Williams is Professor of Contemporary Visual Cultures at the University of Edinburgh. He is the author of eight books including *The Anxious City* (2004), *Brazil: Modern Architectures in History* (2009), *Sex and Buildings* (2013), *Why Cities Look the Way They Do* (2019) and *Reyner Banham Revisited* (2021). He has held fellowships at the Getty Center and the University of São Paulo, and was a British Academy/Leverhulme Senior Research Fellow in 2024 for his project on the imaginaries and futures of urban expressways.

Mimi Zeiger
Mimi Zeiger is a Los Angeles-based critic, editor and curator. Zeiger cocurated the US Pavilion at the 2018 Venice Architecture Biennale and Exhibit Columbus in 2020–21. She has curated and contributed to various exhibitions, and her writing appears in publications including the *New York Times*, *Los Angeles Times*, *The Architectural Review*, *Aperture*, *Wallpaper** and *Metropolis*. Zeiger is the author of multiple books on design, guest editor of the *Los Angeles Review of Architecture*, and serves as the book editor for *Landscape Architecture Magazine*.

Ludovico Centis
Acknowledgements

The conception of this book derives from a six-year-long research and exhibition project that I initiated in 2018, titled *Reyner Banham: A Set of Actual Tracks*. It is in particular the outcome of a symposium held at the Architectural Association (AA) School of Architecture in London on 4 March 2022, titled *What Happens on your 100th Birthday? A Set of Confabulations in Memory of Peter Reyner Banham*, which I organised in collaboration with the AA and The Bartlett School of Architecture at University College London to celebrate the 100th birthday of the British critic and historian.

    I would like to thank Maristella Casciato and the Getty Research Institute for the great support they gave me in the initial phases of the research. The founders of Campo Space in Rome – Gianfranco Bombaci, Matteo Costanzo, Luca Galofaro and Davide Sacconi – gave me the opportunity to first produce an exhibition on Banham in June 2019, titled *A Parallel of Ruins and Landscapes*. A few months later, in September 2019, the symposium and exhibition *They Must Have Enjoyed Building Here: Reyner Banham and Buffalo* was inaugurated at the State University of New York at Buffalo, where Banham taught between 1976 and 1980 and where I was Peter Reyner Banham Fellow for the 2013–14 academic year. This event was made possible by former Dean Robert Shibley, the current and former chairs – Korydon Smith and Omar Khan respectively – and faculty of the School of Architecture and Planning of the State University of New York at Buffalo, including Joyce Hwang, Dennis Maher, Lynda Schneekloth and Hadas Steiner.

    I would like then to thank the former director of the AA, Eva Franch i Gilabert, for introducing me to the fantastic group of people who have sustained me in these past years in running a Visiting School and organising the symposium: Christopher Pierce, Jolene

Malek, Beatriz Chivite and all at the AA Visiting School; Manijeh Verghese and the whole team behind the Public Programme, as well as Maria Shéhérazade Giudici, Edward Bottoms and the AA Archives.

I would also like to thank all the faculty at the Bartlett who took part in the planning of the symposium, and in particular Barbara Penner, Mario Carpo, Adrian Forty and Bob Sheil, as well as all the speakers who generously engaged in duets on themes key to Banham's life and intellectual legacy.

Prior to the symposium, Giovanna Borasi, Shumi Bose, Cynthia Davidson, Davide Tommaso Ferrando, Adrian Forty, Fabrizio Gallanti, Joaquim Moreno, Rory Sherlock and Gianpiero Venturini took part in a week-long discussion with participants Juan R Cantu, Andrew Copolov, Wilson Fung, Gustavo Garcia Vaca, Diego Grisaleña Albéniz, Sheer Gritzerstein, Seonwoo Kim and Punya Sehmi, in the frame of *The Time and Place of Your Life: Online*, an AA Visiting School that was intended as a sequel of *The Time and Place of Your Life*, a course taught by Reyner Banham with Adrian Forty at the Bartlett at the beginning of the 1970s.

I was incredibly lucky to gain deep and exceptional insights into the life and intellectual legacy of Banham thanks to a series of in-person interviews I conducted over past years with artists, architects and scholars who met and worked with Banham in different capacities, periods and contexts. This heterogeneous group includes his son Ben Banham, Edward Ruscha, Adrian Forty, Beverly Foit-Albert, Vittorio Gregotti, Cesare de Seta, François Dallegret, Norman Foster and Roger Conover, who also kindly provided his private correspondence with Banham for the exhibition held at the State University of New York at Buffalo in 2019.

Financial support has been provided by the Getty Research Institute with a 2018 Getty Library Research

Grant and by the Paul Mellon Centre for Studies in British Art with a 2020 Research Support Grant. The production of this book would have been impossible without the encouragement of the Banham family – Ben and Debby Banham and Oliver Arditi – and the support of the current director of the AA, Ingrid Schroder, as well as the AA Publications team – Ryan Dillon, Max Zarzycki and Caspar Bailey.

Finally, I would like to thank Stephanie Davidson, Greg Delaney, Jordan Geiger, Joan Linder, Bruce Majkowski, Timothy Noble, William Offhaus, Miriam Paeslack, Georg Rafailidis, Rick Smith and Jin Young Song in Buffalo, New York, Daniele Pisani at Politecnico di Milano, Francesca Benedetto and Mark Lee at Harvard University (GSD), Mason White at the University of Toronto, Lorenzo Fabian, Sara Marini, Ezio Micelli and Paola Viganò at Università Iuav di Venezia, Sara Basso, Matteo D'Ambros and Elena Marchigiani at Università degli Studi di Trieste, Juan Herreros at Escuela Técnica Superior de Arquitectura de Madrid, Verena von Beckerath at the Bauhaus-Universität Weimar, Thomas Kelley, Francesco Marullo and Florencia Rodriguez at the University of Illinois Chicago, Alessandra Ponte at Université de Montréal and Matthew Coolidge, Curt Gambetta, Todd Gannon, Stefano Graziani, Richard Misrach, Tommaso Petrosino, Elizabeth Selby and Tim Street-Porter for their valuable intellectual exchange and support in different forms throughout these years.

My wife Ilaria and my family shared this journey and encouraged me tirelessly throughout the development of the research.

My son Giorgio was born and has grown up in parallel with the conception and development of the research. I hope he will one day feel curiosity and pleasure in leafing through these pages.

Credits

Every effort has been made to trace copyright holders and obtain permission to reproduce the images and text featured in this publication.

Text by Reyner Banham:

14–20	Copyright © Reyner Banham, 1969. First published in *New Society*, 18 December 1969, pp 986–7.
25–46	Copyright © Reyner Banham, 1965. First published in *Industrial Design*, no 12, September 1965, pp 48–59.
51–64	Copyright © Reyner Banham, 1969. First published in *ARK – Journal of the Royal College of Art*, no 44, 1969, pp 2–11.
76–91	Copyright © Reyner Banham, 1971. First published in *Los Angeles: The Architecture of Four Ecologies* (Penguin, 1971), pp 110–35.
95–105	Copyright © Reyner Banham, 1971. First published in *Los Angeles: The Architecture of Four Ecologies*, pp 213–22.
111–23	Copyright © Reyner Banham, 1971. First published in *Los Angeles: The Architecture of Four Ecologies*, pp 94–109.
130–52	Reyner Banham, *A Concrete Atlantis: U.S. Industrial Building and European Modern Architecture*, pp 1–21 © 1986 Massachusetts Institute of Technology, by permission of The MIT Press.
156–62	Copyright © Reyner Banham, 1983. First published in *New Society*, 5 May 1983, pp 188–9.
166	Copyright © Reyner Banham, 1982. First published in *Scenes in America Deserta* (Gibbs M Smith and Thames and Hudson, 1982), p 68.
173–80	Copyright © Reyner Banham, 1983. First published in *New Society*, 17 March 1983, pp 430–1.
185–95	Copyright © Reyner Banham, 1980. First published in *New West*, 22 September 1980, pp 47–51.
199–206	Copyright © Reyner Banham, 1982. First published in *Scenes in America Deserta*, pp 220–8.

Images:

17	Mies van der Rohe © DACS 2024.
36–7	Courtesy of the Jeep® brand.
38	Courtesy of Polaroid.
57–64	Royal College of Art archive.
66	Copyright © Reyner Banham, 1978. Courtesy of the Architectural Association Archives.
67	Copyright © Reyner Banham, 1986. Courtesy of the Architectural Association Archives.
68	Copyright © Reyner Banham, 1978. Courtesy of the Architectural Association Archives.
69	Copyright © Reyner Banham, 1977. Courtesy of the Architectural Association Archives.
70	Copyright © Reyner Banham, 1983. Courtesy of the Architectural Association Archives.
71	Copyright © Reyner Banham, 1980. Courtesy of the Architectural Association Archives.
80	Mike Salisbury.

81	(top) Copyright © Reyner Banham, 1971. First published in *Los Angeles: The Architecture of Four Ecologies*, p 119.
81	(bottom) David Gebhard.
82	Seaver Center for Western History Research, Los Angeles County Museum of Natural History.
84	Ted Organ.
87	Ed Ruscha.
89	Charles Eames © Eames Office, LLC. All rights reserved.
91	Julius Shulman © J Paul Getty Trust. Getty Research Institute, Los Angeles (2004.R.10).
100–1	William Bronson.
103	Photo by Baron Wolman © The Baron Alan Wolman Collection, Rock & Roll Hall of Fame.
105	George Barris.
114	Seaver Center for Western History Research, Los Angeles County Museum of Natural History.
115	Copyright © Reyner Banham, 1971. First published in *Los Angeles: The Architecture of Four Ecologies*, p 100.
117–8	Spence Air Photos, courtesy of The Benjamin and Gladys Thomas Air Photo Archives.
120	(top) Marvin Rand archive.
120	(bottom) Julius Shulman © J Paul Getty Trust. Getty Research Institute, Los Angeles (2004.R.10).
121	(top) Copyright © Reyner Banham, 1971. First published in *Los Angeles: The Architecture of Four Ecologies*, p 108.
121	(bottom) Julius Shulman © J Paul Getty Trust. Getty Research Institute, Los Angeles (2004.R.10).
122	Julius Shulman © J Paul Getty Trust. Getty Research Institute, Los Angeles (2004.R.10).
132	From the Jahrbuch des Deutschen Werkbundes, 1913.
138	Copyright © Reyner Banham, 1986. First published in *A Concrete Atlantis: U.S. Industrial Building and European Modern Architecture* (MIT Press, 1986), p 5.
139	Erich Mendelsohn.
142–7	From the Jahrbuch des Deutschen Werkbundes, 1913.
149	Erich Mendelsohn.
151	(top) From the Jahrbuch des Deutschen Werkbundes, 1913.
151	(bottom) Patricia Layman Bazelon.
176–7	Copyright © Reyner Banham, 1982. Courtesy of the Architectural Association Archives.
184–95	Tim Street-Porter.